The Guide For Entrepreneurs

GROWING YOUR BUSINESS INTERNATIONALLY

How To Form Profitable Overseas Partnerships, Alliances And Joint Ventures

Marvin V. Bedward & Mark V. Anderson

PROBUS PUBLISHING COMPANY
Chicago, Illinois
Cambridge, England

ISBN 1-55738-464-9

Printed in the United States of America

IPC

2   3   4   5   6   7   8   9   0

This book is dedicated to Annik, Maya and Antoine.

CONTENTS

PREFACE

The world is undergoing a revolution in competitiveness. Everywhere economic barriers are falling as individual countries band together to form regional trading blocks. The globalization of the world economy, predicted by futurists and economists for decades, has come to pass in a very real sense.

In 1992 the European Economic Community (EC) Single Market officially became the world's largest trading bloc, accounting for approximately 20 percent of all extra-EC trade. Its 342 million consumers offer companies substantial economies of scale, along with unlimited manufacturing and marketing opportunities.

The Asia-Pacific region is an equally formidable trading bloc, housing some of the world's most powerful and rapidly growing economies: Japan, South Korea, Singapore, Hong Kong, Taiwan, and Australia. The cash surplus found in the vaults of most Pacific Rim countries makes them particularly attractive business or investment partners.

Globalization means opportunity: opportunity for North American companies to access new and exciting markets—markets larger than any the world has known. But companies hoping to enter and thrive in these markets require an almost superhuman assortment of strengths, including exceptional research and development departments, manufacturing facilities, financial and human resources, and marketing networks, because European and Asia-Pacific business opportunities tend to appear, and disappear, rapidly.

Globalization means global competition: companies unable to move into markets swiftly, efficiently, and powerfully will find them filled by competitors when they get there. Even North American companies with no global ambitions of their own are increasingly forced to protect their domestic markets from aggressive foreign poaching. Factor in rapidly changing technologies, shortened product lives, and exploding research and development (R&D) costs, and the companies of today are facing truly monumental challenges to survival.

It is not surprising, then, that more and more firms are turning to strategic alliances—partnerships with other companies—to overcome daunting odds and take advantage of new opportunities. Alone, not many companies have the combination of strengths needed to succeed. And those that do are often so huge and unwieldy they are unable to mobilize their resources quickly enough to take advantage of rapidly changing windows of opportunity. Even companies the size of General Motors and Ford are using strategic alliances and joint ventures to compete with smaller, more agile and efficient Japanese and European rivals.

Alliances allow companies to focus on what they do best, while relying on the strengths of one or more partners to access technology, improve productivity, and enter new markets.

Among other reasons for pursuing strategic alliances with Asia-Pacific and European companies, one of the most compelling is the eagerness with which companies from both trading blocs greet alliance overtures from North American firms.

For Asia-Pacific companies, strategic alliances have emerged as a preferred way of penetrating North American markets because American hostility over mounting trade imbalances is making it increasingly difficult for them to pursue their traditional export activities.

Both European and North American companies find strategic alliances perfectly suited to the quickly changing, highly competitive, and varied conditions found in the EC. Because North Americans and Europeans often share a common cultural heritage and similar managerial practices, transatlantic alliances are relatively easy to implement.

Growing Your Business Internationally was written to give North American businessmen an indication of the opportunities that exist in the emerging trading blocs of Europe and the Asia-Pacific area, and to demonstrate how these opportunities can be addressed through the formation and management of strategic alliances.

The book describes ways in which North American companies can access the specific blend of skills and resources they need in order to be competitive in Europe and the Asia-Pacific region. It explains how small and medium-sized companies (SMEs) can use alliances to leverage their strengths through cooperation. Many smaller firms realize they must enter foreign markets if they are to grow and prosper, but on their own they simply do not have the skills or resources to take advantage of international opportunities.

Likewise, *Growing Your Business Internationally* shows how strategic alliances can help large companies bypass their cumbersome infrastructures to achieve the greater flexibility and responsiveness required by today's rapidly changing technologies and markets.

Part I of this book describes what strategic alliances are, how to determine if an alliance is the best strategic option for your company, and how to structure and manage one so that it fulfills the overall objectives of your company.

Chapter 1, "Today's Competitive Challenge," describes the challenges that strategic alliances are designed to meet. It supplies the context for the rest of book.

Chapter 2, "What Do Strategic Alliances Offer?," begins by describing the particular advantages of each type of strategic alliance, from research consortia to joint ventures and cross-licensing agreements. It then focuses on how they can be used to enhance the competitive position of your firm. For example, alliances are effective ways for small firms to achieve economies of scale or to reduce high risks.

Chapter 3, "Is a Strategic Alliance Right for You?," takes you step by step through the issues involved in deciding if a strategic alliance is right for you. This chapter will help you ensure that the strategy your company follows is based on what it needs to fulfill its overall objectives. This chapter discusses how to carry out a strategic audit in order to determine where your company is, where it needs to be, and what it needs in order to get there.

Chapter 4, "Finding the Right Partner," describes what to look for in a strategic partner. It also identifies the danger signs that will warn you if your prospective marriage may not have been formed in heaven.

Chapter 5, "Negotiating a Strategic Alliance," walks you through the steps involved in structuring your agreement. It describes the importance of a carefully thought-out business framework.

Chapter 6, "Managing Your Strategic Alliance," looks at the kind of staff you will need to assign to a partnership, and how to motivate them. It also considers special communication problems involved in coordinating the activities of the alliance partners, and offers important advice on how to resolve conflicts. Finally, it reviews some options for monitoring the performance of an alliance.

Parts II and III of *Growing Your Business Internationally* detail the alliance opportunities to be found in the emerging trading blocks of Europe (EC) and the Asia-Pacific region, respectively. For North American firms seeking new resources, expertise, technology, and markets, there are no better hunting grounds. Penetration of these vast and sophisticated markets will enhance any company's competitive position in the global marketplace.

Success in the European Economic Community Single Market demands an ability to respond rapidly to changing technological and business conditions. Few North American businesses will be able to prosper in the EC if all they do is maintain arms-length relationships. The Asia-Pacific region offers some of the world's most powerful and rapidly developing economies—economies with vast technological and financial resources. It is in these markets that North American companies will have to compete, or die.

The appendices found at the end of the book should be consulted at specific points. Appendix A corresponds to Part I, Chapter 3. It lists the questions you will need to address when carrying out a strategic audit, and it provides you with space to jot down your answers and thoughts as you go along.

Appendix B corresponds to Part I, Chapter 5, and supplements the discussion on structuring a legal framework with an outline of a joint-venture legal agreement.

Throughout this book you will find examples in italics of strategic alliances that are functioning on the global stage. They illustrate both the strengths and weaknesses of alliances and provide you with the background information you will need to assess the value of this business tool in terms of the development of your company into the twenty-first century.

ACKNOWLEDGEMENTS

A book of this nature and scope necessarily involves the cooperation and efforts of many people. We appreciate the valuable contributions made by a number of writers and researchers, many of them associates of the Prospectus Group of Companies—Mr. Arpad Abonyi, M.A., Dr. Michael Kelly, Ms. Katie Reid, B.A., Ms. Dyna Vynk Ellis, M.A., researched the initial material for Part I on Strategic Alliances. Mr. Arpad Abonyi, Dr. Lynn Mytelka and Mr. William Gayner, B.A., researched and wrote much of the material for Part II, and Dr. Jan Fedorowicz researched and wrote much of the material for Part III of the book.

We are immensely grateful to the individuals and corporations who have shared their stories with us, as well as the Governments of Canada, Ontario and Quebec, and the Hongkong Bank of Canada for their support of the research. We especially thank those who read the drafts, including: Dr. Michael Kelly; Roger Hul; McEvoy Galbreath of Prospectus Publications Ltd; and Pamela van Giessen and Carol Barnstable of Probus Publishing Company.

Marvin Bedward
Mark Anderson
Ottawa, Canada

PART I

FORMING AND MANAGING STRATEGIC ALLIANCES

CHAPTER 1

TODAY'S COMPETITIVE CHALLENGE

• ALLIANCES CHANGING THE LANDSCAPE

A New Landscape

In today's rapidly evolving business world, strategic alliances are transforming the landscape. Consortia, new distribution channels, and networks of alliances are all signs of a fundamental change. Firms once proud of their self-sufficiency are now cooperating with other firms. Like atoms that have decided to become molecules, businesses are evolving increasingly complex and interdependent relationships.

Worldwide, the biotechnology industry alone produced at least 624 new technological cooperation agreements between 1980 and 1987, while in the information technology industry more than 1,516 technology-related agreements were created during the same period.

As the structure of whole industries changes, competitive advantage increasingly depends not only on the internal capabilities of a firm, but also on the scope of its relationships with other firms. Strategic alliances are formed by companies cooperating out of mutual need, to achieve goals they could not easily reach on their own. Alliances are powerful tools, and when used properly they afford great flexibility and responsiveness. But, just as with any powerful tool, strategic alliances can be tricky and even dangerous to use—they should never be pursued lightly, impatiently, and without strict attention to detail.

Alliances are demanding, and should only be used by those who are able to invest the time and energy necessary to ensure their proper application and continued maintenance. They vary widely in scope and complexity, from simple licensing agreements to independently functioning joint ventures.

Strategic alliances have become an important part of the vocabulary of most managers. They supply a range of tools that few companies can afford to ignore—even if alliances are not an immediate option.

That was not always the case. Alliances were once commonly viewed as choices of last resort, used by companies for products of secondary importance or to bypass local ownership regulations.

A Small Firm With Global Linkages

Quadra Logic Technologies (QLT) of Vancouver is a small firm with a global perspective. It has developed an international network to sell its anti-cancer drugs and diagnostic products.

QLT's partners include Armard-Frappier, Genentech, Guangdong Enterprises of China, International Minerals and Chemical Corporation, and an Italian distributor. The partnerships cover such areas as joint research and manufacturing as well as distribution and marketing.

Using alliances strategically has meant that even a small company such as QLT can develop sophisticated linkages, with established distribution networks over several continents.

Alliances have arrived—and they are not just another passing fad. Their coming of age is directly related to the major changes that are defining the world in which we live and work. Today, alliances are called "strategic" because their formation is of critical strategic importance to companies.

In the following sections, we will discuss the three major factors that account for this change: the increasing competitiveness of today's markets, the escalating costs of doing business, and the need to penetrate global markets. Strategic alliances provide ways of transforming these challenges into new opportunities.

Today's markets are more competitive than ever before. For North American firms, this heightened competitiveness can be attributed to the emergence of powerful new global competitors such as the Japanese and the newly

Diagram 1   Forms of Alliances

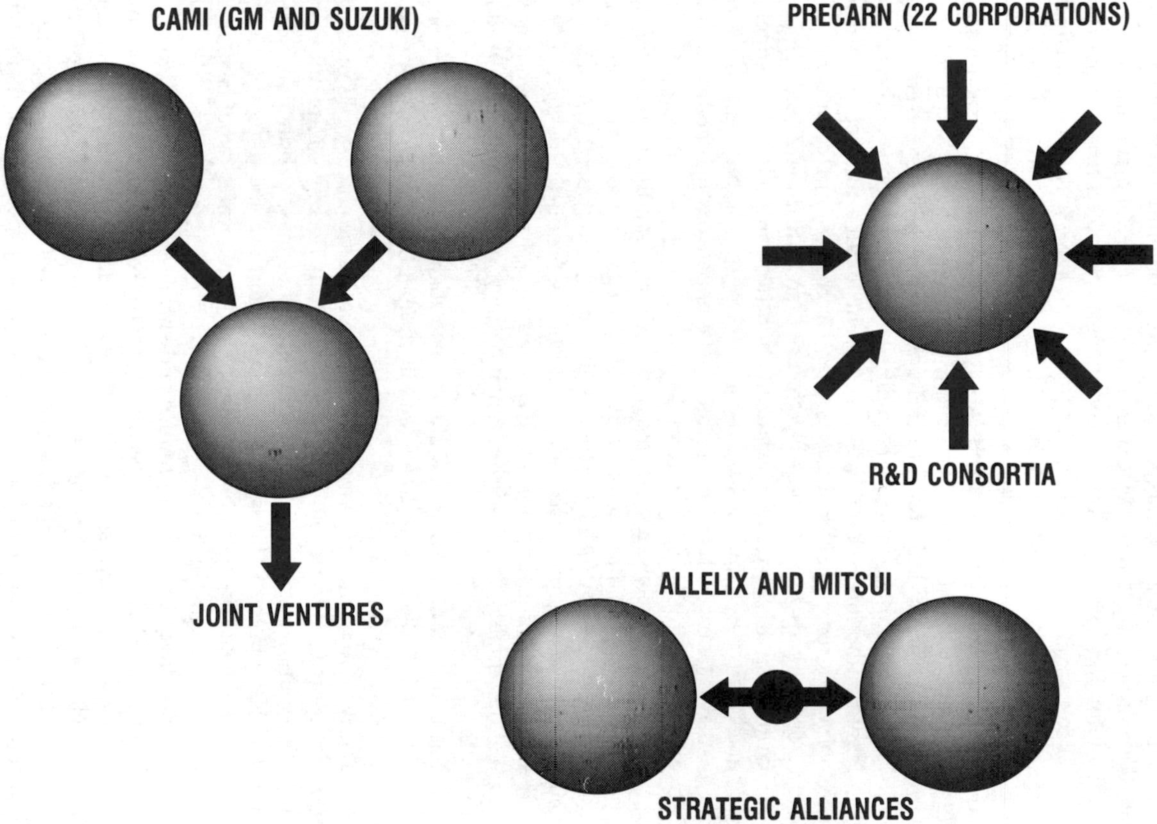

CAMI (GM AND SUZUKI)

JOINT VENTURES

PRECARN (22 CORPORATIONS)

R&D CONSORTIA

ALLELIX AND MITSUI

STRATEGIC ALLIANCES

industrialized four "tigers" of southeast Asia: South Korea, Singapore, Taiwan, and Hong Kong.

Meanwhile, the unification of the European Economic Community is rationalizing EC industries, making them more competitive globally, and increasing the pressure on North American industry. The dramatic inroads already made by foreign companies on this continent have forced firms in the U.S. and Canada to reexamine old assumptions and find new ways of enhancing their products, services, and performance.

Japan became a world economic power by moving up the technological ladder. Japanese companies worked closely with government to secure a powerful position in one sector and then used it as a base to move into another sector with higher technological content. Throughout, the Japanese used knowledge and skills to create innovative, high quality, competitive goods and services.

Now South Korea is following closely in Japan's footsteps. It is already developing a strong position in consumer electronics and computers. In fact, South Korea already exports more electronics than Canada—$2.6 billion in 1986.

Firms from advanced industrialized countries can no longer compete with companies from newly industrialized countries purely on the basis of the cost of inputs such as labor. Today, these firms must compete on their ability to innovate through the exploitation of new technologies.

In textiles, they have moved into high fashion, computerization, and special types of industrial textiles such as materials for spacesuits. In automobiles, they have incorporated advanced electronics into cars, introduced CAD/CAM into their manufacturing processes, and customized products for specific market niches. In consumer electronics, Western companies have focused on innovative design, high quality, sophisticated engineering, and CAD/CAM production processes.

The nature of economies of scale has also changed. In the 1960s, economies of scale were usually enough to ensure the competitiveness of a company. After all, competition was not as fierce.

Today, many firms in many countries can mass-produce goods more cheaply than can be done in developed countries. In this fiercely competitive market, companies can no longer rely on the advantages of mass production alone. The important issue in the 1990s is not size per se, but how you deploy your resources. It is no longer enough to produce in the right quantities, what is vital is how you organize your production.

It is no longer enough to produce and ship large quantities of goods overseas. Today, global competitiveness requires sensitivity to local markets. Supplier and distribution networks are growing more complex and their proper orchestration is vital. The use of appropriate technologies and the layout of production systems are also key issues. And as industry becomes more technologically intensive, fewer people are involved in the production process—but their technical skills and cultural flexibility will be taxed as the pace of change and the demand to interact with other cultures and new ideas increase.

Diagram 2   International Competition

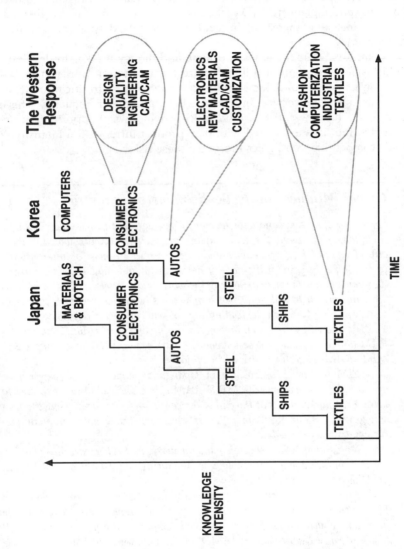

In order to stay competitive, Western firms have to climb the technology ladder, investing in R&D, improving their products, services, and performance. This means that, for many firms investing in the development of new products and technologies, the cost of doing business has increased dramatically.

To develop a new generation of technology today requires quantum leaps in complexity and ingenuity. R&D costs no longer rise arithmetically, they rise geometrically: instead of increasing in regular increments, they spiral upward in ever steeper curves.

Ironically, while the amount of time and money it takes to develop a new product is increasing, product lifetimes are getting shorter. Under the pressure of technological change and competition, companies are introducing new and improved products and services into the market with greater frequency. This means that products become outdated more quickly, windows of opportunity grow narrower, and the risks associated with new product introduction intensify. Yet, to remain competitive, companies must take these risks.

Global Alliances in the Semiconductor Industry

For a long time semiconductor memory chips have been the subject of bitter trade tension between the U.S., Japan and Europe. Today, however, these critical computer components are the center of a number of international partnerships, in spite of the fiercely nationalistic and independent nature of the semiconductor industry. Some of the world's largest electronics companies are being driven to collaborative arrangements by increasing costs and risks associated with being on the leading edge of semiconductor technology.

Partnerships are becoming increasingly common in the $7 billion D-RAM (dynamic random access memory) market, with R&D costs of the 256 MB D-RAMs expected to exceed $1 billion.

IBM in the U.S., Toshiba in Japan and Seimens of Germany have agreed to jointly develop 256 MB D-RAM chips. These chips are expected to make their market debut at the end of the century. While the current partnership focuses only on R&D, many experts feel that it will move into manufacturing at some future date.

NEC, Japan's largest semiconductor maker and AT&T are also working together on the advanced technology for the future generations of D-RAMs as are Hitachi and Texas Instruments.

Another area involving high costs and risks is flash memory technology. Flash memory devices are expected to eventually replace disk drives as the data storage medium for portable personal computers and facsimile machines.

Advance Micro Devices (AMD) of the U.S. and Futjitsu of Japan are spending $700 million for a 50/50 joint venture to manufacture flash memory devices. AMD had the flash memory technology but lacked the resources to build its own facility of the scale required. Fujitsu, on the other hand lacked *the technology, but had the semiconductor manufacturing expertise, the capital and access to the Japanese market. By pooling their resources, the two companies will be able to establish a larger scale facility capable of producing 20,000 eight-inch semiconductor wafers a month, allowing for substantial economies of scale and establishing a very tough competitive standard.*

Because of these pressures, the rules of corporate survival have changed, and a whole body of widely accepted knowledge concerning corporate strategies has virtually been thrown out the window.

Traditionally, companies pursued a strategy of vertical integration and diversification. They created complex networks of centrally controlled satellite plants, foreign subsidiaries, suppliers of key inputs, and peripheral businesses. But companies are finding that such structures are expensive, hard to manage, and unwieldy. They lack the flexibility needed in a highly competitive and fast-changing environment.

Instead, corporations are focusing on their core businesses. They are spinning off peripheral activities, in-house suppliers, uneconomic plants, and unprofitable subsidiaries. By sticking to what they do best, they preserve their competitiveness in a demanding world.

Diagram 3   Escalating Costs in the Mega Chip Race

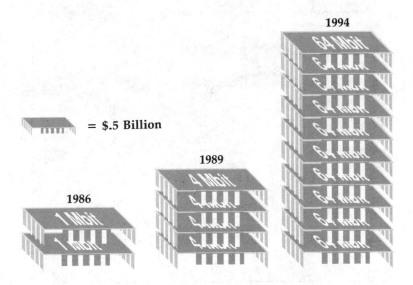

Strategic alliances enable firms to leverage their special strengths into larger markets and more diversified areas. They enable firms to share the high costs and risks of business. And they provide firms with ways to access new technologies, expertise, large capital resources, and new markets—without creating the monolithic corporate structures that are so hard to manage.

Business is going global. Improved telecommunication and transportation links are ushering in a new era of international interdependence. New countries are entering the industrialized world and new markets are opening up.

All over the world, governments are attempting to make it easier for their businesses to take advantage of larger markets. Canada and the United States have the Free Trade Agreement (FTA), while among Mexico, the U.S.A. and Canada, a trilateral North American Free Trade Agreement (NAFTA) is currently being negotiated. The European Economic Community Single Market has been inaugurated, the former East Bloc countries are opening their economies to foreign investment, and there is talk of greater economic cooperation among Pacific Rim countries.

The escalating costs of business are a major reason firms are taking advantage of international markets. Increasingly, domestic markets are no longer large enough to generate the profits needed to pay for sky-rocketing development costs or to underwrite the high risks of introducing new products with short life spans. In order to achieve the necessary economies of scale, firms must enter

Diagram 4   From National to International Markets

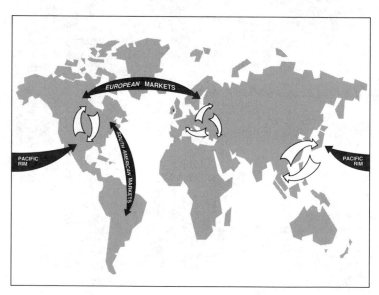

global markets. (For further discussion of the issue, see the section on economies of scale in Chapter 2.)

Today, both small and large companies are recognizing the need to become globally competitive. Growing foreign investment and market penetration means that whether a company expands beyond its local market or not, it will be competing with companies from all over the world, companies that have grown strong by taking advantage of global opportunities.

The situation is particularly acute for mid-sized firms. They can be dangerously outclassed, because they do not have the internal resources of their larger rivals. They need international investment strategies to position themselves effectively in global markets. They also need ways of leveraging their business strengths and financial power.

Strategic alliances provide a variety of ways for companies to access the resources necessary to enter foreign markets. These vary from participating in overseas joint ventures, to exchanges of products through cross-licensing agreements. What these methods share in common is the ability to provide firms with the technology, capital, or market access they need in order to enter foreign markets, which they might not be able to afford or achieve on their own.

CHAPTER 2

WHAT DO STRATEGIC ALLIANCES OFFER?

- FOCUS ON STRENGTHS
- COMPETITIVE TOOLS
- TYPES OF ALLIANCES
- R&D ALLIANCES ON THE RISE
- SETTING STANDARDS

Strategic Alliances Focus on Strengths

Business people are learning they cannot be all things to all people, and the most competitive corporations stick to what they do best. At the same time, the boundaries separating different industrial and scientific fields have blurred as technology has advanced. More and more often, projects require the coordination of expertise from fields that once had little in common.

Strategic alliances allow firms to focus on their own strengths, while cooperating with other companies to get a job done. They allow firms to leverage, expand, and become profitable in various business areas without investing huge amounts of time or energy.

Properly focused, and with a well-defined set of objectives, strategic alliances offer great responsiveness and flexibility. Using alliances, even small firms can compete in varied markets. The linkages formed are restricted by the company's ability to manage the linkages, rather than by its capital resources. The ability to approach several markets at once with similar products provides the company with a much better likelihood of recovering its initial investment before its products become obsolete.

Benzon Pharma Focuses on Its Strengths

Benzon Pharma is a small Danish drug company that is part of Alfred Benzon, the health-care and consumer-goods group. With sales of US $20 million, Benzon Pharma's sales are tiny compared to the billions of dollars that the British giant Glaxo or the Anglo-American Smith-Kline Beecham sell each year.

Most drug companies have three stages of activities: research, development, and marketing. Development costs—requiring repeated clinical trials on thousands of patients—are very high. Development costs of US $114 million are not unusual.

Benzon has chosen to skip the development stage altogether, leaving it to the giants who can more easily afford it. This has enabled it to focus on its special strengths in research and marketing. All of its research projects are carried out with an eye to linking them to the projects of much larger companies. Half of Benzon's sales derive from the fruits of research projects, which are sold to larger companies. The other half comes from sales of products tested and patented by other companies.

The company has leveraged these activities through a number of alliances with other companies. For example, Scherling-Plough of the United States and Celltech of the United Kingdom have cooperative agreements through which they gain access to the new biotechnology developed by Benzon. Benzon also has a licensing agreement with the Swiss giant Ciba-Geigy.

When Are Strategic Alliances Competitive Tools?

Strategic alliances can be used as tools to enhance the competitiveness of firms, enabling them to respond faster to competition, increase market share, solve technological problems, protect sources of competitive advantage, and supplement internal resources and capabilities, when:

- the strategic objectives for the alliance are clear

- the partners are committed to objectives and focus on cooperation
- the alliance is efficiently organized and managed
- the capabilities of the partners complement each other
- partners are well-informed and have reasonable expectations

Alliances Are Used to:

- develop new industries
- revitalize established industries
- rationalize a firm's activities
- enhance competitive advantage in a particular area

Types of Strategic Alliances

Strategic alliances offer a wide selection of arrangements. All of them can pull companies together, forming linkages that enable firms to pool ideas and resources, keep pace with market changes, reduce risk, and move into new market areas.

Agreements between firms may call for the transfer of technology, cooperation on research or product development, or the exchange of marketing rights. Sometimes, firms provide equity to form a new, free-standing company—a joint venture.

Types of Strategic Alliances Include:

- Joint Research and Development
- Cross-Manufacturing Agreements
- Co-marketing or Co-promotion Agreements
- Licensing Agreements
- Cross-Licensing Agreements

Joint Research and Development

Joint research and development projects are an effective strategy to reduce financial risks and access expertise. They also allow firms to invest in a variety of development efforts, instead of being trapped—due to a lack of resources—into putting all their eggs in one basket.

Joint R&D has become a very common strategy in the computer industry. R&D costs are high, and, with competition within the industry more intense than ever, manufacturers' margins are being squeezed. As a result, only a few companies can afford to carry out R&D for advanced applications by themselves.

Joint R&D efforts are also a good way to combine the resources of firms, governments, universities, and consortia. In addition, Joint R&D projects often reap unexpected benefits in the form of new perspectives and fresh insights.

Joint R&D is most commonly found in basic research or applied research in the stages before a new product is commercialized.

R&D Consortia

Companies around the world are forming teams to share R&D skills and expenses. For example, in the United States, IBM, Hewlett-Packard, Texas Instruments, and others have formed a research consortium called Sematech to do basic research into semiconductors.

In Canada, 20 companies are cooperating through the PRECARN consortium to find ways of using robotics and artificial intelligence in the mining and materials industries.

In Europe, organizations such as ESPRIT and RACE offer companies throughout the EC opportunities to cooperate in order to develop information technologies and telecommunications.

Companies are pairing off for R&D too. The Canadian drug company Apotex Inc. and ABI Biotechnology (Canada) have formed a joint technology development agreement. Apotex contributes its financing and worldwide distribution capabilities, while ABI brings its technical expertise. Apotex invested $11.4 million in ABI and will finance the construction of a $20 to $25 million manufacturing facility in Winnipeg. ABI will build the plant and develop and manufacture the pharmaceuticals. As the exclusive distributor, Apotex takes over at that point, marketing the products worldwide.

In 1984, Philips NV of the Netherlands and Siemens AG of Germany started Megaproject in order to develop the next generation of superchips. Texaco, Inc. and LeCarbone-Lorraine (LCL) of France plan to enter a joint research and technical support agreement in order to develop synthetic membranes for use in separation processes. Similarly, Allelix of Canada and Mitsui Petrochemicals of Japan have an agreement to develop anti-cancer drugs.

Joint Ventures

A joint venture is an independent business formed through the cooperation of two or more parent firms. Joint ventures have been used traditionally for entering foreign markets to avoid ownership restrictions. While this is still a popular and effective strategy, today companies find many more uses for joint ventures than simply getting around government regulations.

The central characteristic of a joint venture is that it is an equity-based relationship. Each parent has equity in the joint venture and is represented on the board of directors. This means joint ventures are more complicated to end than are other forms of strategic alliances. And because they are separate entities, organizing and managing joint ventures requires special consideration.

Since they involve added complications, forming a joint venture with another firm makes sense only if the nature of the project requires commitments from the partners that go beyond the legal forms of a contractual agreement.

If the ownership of the joint venture is split 50-50, it is usually because the partners are about the same size and both want a large say in the company. Unequal ownership usually reflects an unequal contribution of resources by the parent companies.

Suzuki Invests in Hungarian Auto Industry

Hungary's passenger-car industry, dormant for half a century, got a boost with the formal launch of a joint venture to produce 50,000 Suzuki cars a year by 1995. The $230 million project unites Suzuki Motor Co. Ltd., the Hungarian consortium Autokonszern Inc, C. Itoh and Co. Ltd., and World Bank affiliate International Finance Corporation (IFC). Suzuki and Autokonszern will each have 40 percent stakes in Magyar Suzuki Co., based in Esztergom, and capitalized at $73 million. C. Itoh will own 11 percent and IFC 9 percent.

Magyar Suzuki, Hungary's largest joint venture, will produce 16,000 five-door hatchback Swifts with 1.0- and 1.3-liter engines by 1994, with capacity rising to 60,000 after five years. The joint venture marks Japanese automakers' first foothold in Eastern Europe, which is expected to be one of the fastest-growing markets for cars in the next decade.

Licensing Agreements

In a licensing agreement, a single firm licenses its products or services to one or more firms. For example, Marubeni Corp. and Kurabo Industries have both signed licensing agreements with Clonetics Corporation of San Diego. The agreements give Marubeni and Kurabo exclusive Japanese marketing rights to two kits developed by Clonetics for use in biochemical research.

In another example of a licensing agreement, Immunomedics Inc. received funding from Johnson & Johnson's Ortho Diagnostic Systems (Canada). In return, Ortho has received the exclusive Canadian distribution rights to serum tests Immunomedics has developed to detect and monitor autoimmune diseases such as lupus, rheumatoid arthritis, AIDS, and AIDS-related complex.

Licensing transfers no property rights, only usage rights, so the licensor still has some control over the product. Issues that are subject to negotiation include royalties, patents, sublicensing possibilities, rights to sell and manufacture, time length and geographical limitations of the license, the issue of exclusivity, and issues revolving around the updating of technology.

Cross-licensing

Cross-licensing is a strategic alliance between two firms in which each licenses products or services to the other. Today, companies are, in effect, exchanging the rights to use their products or services with each other.

For example, one of South Korea's largest electronics companies, Samsung Electronics Co., signed a cross-licensing agreement with IBM Korea Inc. in 1989. The agreement granted each company complete access to the other's patents for technology used in the design and manufacture of semiconductor products.

Both licensing and cross-licensing are relatively straightforward ways for companies to share products or expertise without the complications of more-intense collaboration. However, because they involve less cooperation, they hold a lesser promise of synergy—the happy situation where cooperation results in benefits greater than the sum of each company's investment.

Cross-Manufacturing

Cross-manufacturing agreements are a form of cross-licensing in which companies agree to manufacture each other's products.

Co-Marketing or Co-Promotion

In co-marketing or co-promotion agreements, companies market or promote each other's products. An agreement could involve cross-licensing, a shared promotion campaign, or even the formation of a joint venture to market their products. Most do not involve licenses or royalties, but some rights to the product may be worked into the agreement.

The first significant co-promotion deal in the drug industry was between Glaxo and Hoffman-LaRoche in 1983, to market Zantac, an anti-ulcer drug. In 1988, they agreed to co-market Ceftin, an oral antibiotic.

For firms wanting to enter new markets, co-marketing agreements are an effective way to take advantage of existing distribution networks and to access local market knowledge. They allow firms whose products are complementary to fill out a product line while avoiding expensive and time-consuming development.

Joint Production

In joint-production agreements, companies cooperate in order to produce goods. These agreements enable firms to share complementary resources and take advantage of economies of scale. Companies may cooperate to make components, or even entire products.

Many engineering firms have entered into joint production agreements with firms with manufacturing expertise, while, in the auto and the telecommunications industries, it is common for competing firms to form an alliance to make components needed by all.

East Meets West Through Co-Production

The automotive industry is weaving a complex web of interconnections. There are several co-production agreements involving Japanese companies in the US:

Mazda's Flat Rock, Michigan, car plant is the fruit of a production agreement with Ford. The plant produces the Ford Probe, the Mazda MX-6, and the Mazda 626. Mazda contributed its engineering capabilities and Ford its knowledge and access to North American markets. Ford also owns 20 to 25 percent of Mazda.

Ford and Nissan are designing and building a minivan together. Nissan is primarily responsible for the engineering, and Ford will handle the manufacturing. Too small to go it alone, Subaru and Isuzu have united to form SIAM—Subaru-Isuzu of America Manufacturing. Their plant in Indiana produces a line from each company, and a shared minivan is in development.

Strategic alliances can be used in a variety of ways. For many companies, strategic alliances provide an important way of achieving the critical mass and achieving the economies of scale they need for success.

Strategic alliances are also useful for repositioning a firm in the marketplace. When one market starts to fade away, a company can free up resources by forming

Diagram 5   Competitive Alliances in the Auto Industry

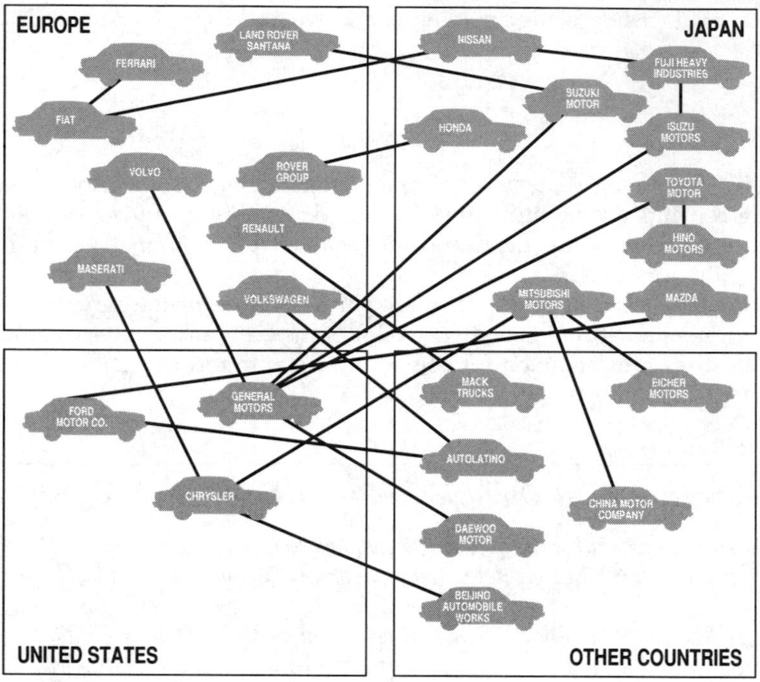

Source: Delvin &Bleackley, Strategic Alliances—Guidelines for Success, October 1988.

existing customers. The firm might then form a new alliance in another business area to take advantage of complementary resources.

In the end, strategic alliances are about leveraging strengths by accessing the skills or resources of other firms through cooperation. Their successful outcome depends on the commitment of the partners to get the appropriate resources and skilled personnel strategic alliances need.

A strategic alliance may be the best way—or the only way—for your firm to acquire the skills or resources it requires. Often, when companies get together to share specialized expertise, they are exchanging skills that are not available for sale. Companies often prefer to leverage their technology into a larger business, rather than sell or lease it for a fixed amount. Or the technology might be so new or sophisticated as to make it difficult to package for sale or lease. And, of course, the expertise may be embodied in the key people within a company.

On the Defensive

Some firms enter alliances in order to defend their market position. This can be true of even very large companies. For instance, when Westinghouse lost its 40 percent share of the U.S. market in high-voltage circuit breakers, it joined with Mitsubishi Electric Corp. Within a year, it had regained 15 percent of the market.

Similarly, Clark Equipment of the United States combined its earth-moving business with Volvo of Sweden in order to generate enough sales volume for both of them to survive in the face of competition from world leaders such as Caterpillar and Komatsu.

Many partnerships are struck between large and small firms. Typically, the small firm possesses technological expertise and the ability to keep abreast of fast-changing technologies and markets. The large partner needs this technology, and finds that it no longer has the flexibility or drive to remain on the cutting edge. What the large partner may have is vast amounts of capital, large distribution systems, a lot of market savvy, and instant credibility. Each, then, provides the other with vital resources.

Skills and Resources Accessible Through Strategic Alliances

- Technology

- Marketing and Contacts

- Management

- Sources of Financing

- Distribution Networks

- Servicing Networks

- Consulting, Various In-House Systems

A Small Company Leads the Project

Simon Standley knew it was a good idea—but he also suspected that his company might need partners to get the job done. Standley is managing director of Precision Systems, a small British company that specializes in advanced welding. The new product was capable of automatically regrinding the worn edges of turbine blades in jet engines. With only 12 employees and a turnover of US $1 million, Precision Systems lacked the money and diverse skills to develop and market the equipment successfully.

Standley found the right partners through BRITE (the Basic Research in Industrial Technology for Europe program). All three partners are German. Isotopen-Technik is a small supplier of image-processing software; Aachen Technical University will supply the alliance with expertise in the field of sensors; and the German Nuclear Energy Research center will supply the X-ray technology. The European Commission is providing US $1.6 million of the $3.3 million cost of the four-year project, with $600,000 going to the British company, which will act as project leader even though it is the smallest of the partners.

Strategic alliances have been used for over 50 years as a vehicle for entering international markets. Traditionally, they provided a way for firms to satisfy government regulations concerning minimum local ownership. International companies were able to maintain a large equity stake in the business while taking advantage of local expertise. They also provided a way for local companies in less-developed countries to learn more-effective business techniques from their foreign partners.

These reasons still hold true. Joint ventures remain the preferred means for entry into India, the former Soviet republics, Africa, and eastern Europe, for example.

But with the importance of global markets in today's business world, joint ventures and other forms of strategic alliances with overseas partners have come into their own for more reasons than satisfying local ownership criteria.

A study of American business showed that over 50 percent of high-growth manufacturing companies in the U.S. used non-trade modes of entry into foreign markets. In the service industry, this figure was virtually 100 percent. Instead of simply exporting, more and more companies are turning to strategic alliances, mergers and acquisitions, or greenfield investment to penetrate foreign markets.

Strategic alliances are effective ways of entering new markets, be they domestic or international. Partners can provide already-established marketing and distribution systems, as well as knowledge of the markets they serve. They ensure that products get to market more quickly and more effectively.

In addition, foreign partners can give valuable advice on how to modify a product to meet local regulations and market preferences. They can help with such issues as translation of documentation, conversion between metric and English units of measure, conversion of power requirements, and complying with packaging regulations.

With an eye to the competition, companies often cooperate in marketing or distribution. By anticipating a new situation, it is possible to preempt the competition. A well-conceived alliance could mean a head start in a market, possibly even preventing other competitors from entering. And allying with a heavy-weight can sweep smaller competitors away.

Strategic alliances can also be used to defend against intrusive competition. One of the benefits of cross-distribution agreements, for instance, is that both partners avoid competing with each other in the specified markets.

High Stake Alliances: Testing for AIDS and Profit

Companies have combined forces in order to profit in the growing AIDS diagnostics market. Abbott Laboratories and DuPont control a lion's portion, while many of the major multinationals—such as Baxter Healthcare Corp., Eastman Kodak Co., and Organon Teknika—are hedging their bets through alliances with smaller companies.

The smaller firms contribute the expertise to develop the test and to adapt it to a specific market niche, while the larger partner provides the substantial capital and marketing resources needed to establish a presence in AIDS testing.

A few smaller firms are forming partnerships, most often to enable experts in different technologies to combine forces. Deals between large firms in the field are usually struck to access overseas marketing and distribution channels. For example, Abbott has a joint venture with Dainippon Pharmaceutical Co. Ltd., one of the oldest pharmaceutical companies in Japan, to market Abbott's products in that country.

Popularity of R&D Alliances on the Rise

Risk reduction through strategic alliances is most clearly seen in R&D areas, where the scale and complexity of developing new technology, products, and markets is increasing in quantum leaps.

Competition is fiercer than it ever was. R&D costs are spiraling upward, and the speed of innovation means that products quickly become outdated. Sharing R&D costs and facilities provides good value for the money, while sharing expertise can create synergies that dramatically speed up the whole process.

Cooperating in R&D is particularly important to firms that want to stay on top of several research areas. By doing some in-house research along one track and cooperative research along other tracks, a firm can diversify itself across several possibilities without putting as much of its resources at risk.

As important as cooperation between firms has become in R&D, strategic alliances are now used to decrease risks in any area that is of vital interest to a business. Sharing established distribution systems, for instance, saves money and guarantees the delivery of the product in a fraction of the time—an important point as the life expectancy of products falls.

The importance of strategic alliances to high-tech companies simply highlights their growing importance to all industries. The problems high-tech companies began wrestling with yesterday are the problems that face the rest of us today. The importance of strategic alliances in addressing high-tech challenges

Diagram 6   Competitive Alliances in Telecommunications

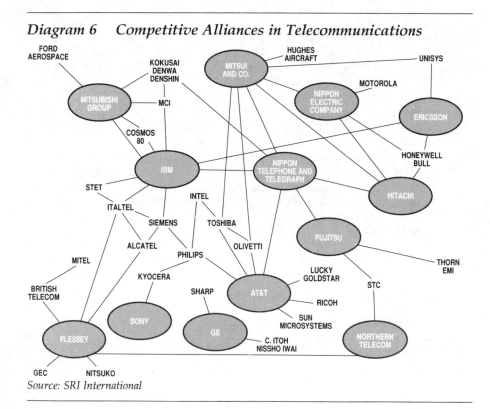

Source: SRI International

indicates that business in general may soon be alliance-based. Failure to understand how to use strategic alliances to their full potential may be the biggest risk of all.

MIPS Completely Restructures Itself

"We would walk into a company like General Motors, tell them we were a $12 million business, and ask them to bet a piece of their future on us," remembers Robert Miller, president of Silicon Valley prodigy MIPS Computer Systems. "That is a tough sell."

MIPS was floundering. It had the right product, but it didn't have the size needed to convince large corporations like GM that it could fulfill their needs. MIPS had to expand, but it was having problems drawing the necessary investors. After a weekend of brainstorming, company leaders finally decided to completely restructure the company using strategic alliances.

Needed: high-quality, high-volume, state-of-the-art production capabilities. In short order, Miller had formed partnerships with three top domestic producers—LSI Logic, Integrated Device Technology, and Performance Semiconductor—as well as international manufacturers Siemens of West Germany and NEC of Japan.

Next, he wove a tapestry of alliances with 20 companies, ensuring that MIPS-based systems would get wide distribution with strong service to customers. These partnerships usually involve close R&D cooperation but—unlike the production agreements—are easy to terminate. The 20 companies include Digital Equipment, Tandem Computers, Prime Computers, and Sony. It was the first time industry heavyweight Digital Equipment had ever gone outside for important new technology.

Source: Business Month, Sept. 1989.

Setting Standards

The development of new technologies creates entirely new market opportunities. And the company that is the first to create a new technology may set the standards for its industry simply by virtue of being the first one there while everybody else is still trying to catch up.

Today, however, several competitors may well develop similar technologies around the same time. Since it is very difficult to predict whose technology will set the standard for the industry, trying to be the first into the market with a new technology can be a very risky game. If someone else's product sets the standard for the industry, you can easily be cut out of the market. And with today's high costs of R&D, the stakes in these games can be frighteningly high.

Philips Learned It the Hard Way . . .

International standards can make or break a product. When Japanese manufacturers managed to establish worldwide video standards that were not compatible with Philips' technology, Philips was driven out of the market.

When Philips entered the compact-disc market, it took steps to make sure it would not get frozen out again. It entered into strategic alliances with Sony and DuPont for CD development and production. It also licensed its CD technology to other companies at a low fee to encourage demand. As a result, Philips has a prominent position in the CD market.

Today, standards are the basis by which a new market is established. Risk sharing and windows on leading-edge developments are good reasons for cooperation, but when new standards are involved, the most important reason to cooperate with others is to increase the odds that the standards that you have invested in will be accepted throughout the industry. Standards make markets, and for this reason, many high-technology companies cannot afford not to be involved in some sort of alliance, consortium, or other cooperative effort.

In the telecommunications industry, for example, competitors have collaborated to create a new international set of standards for the Integrated Services Digital Network (ISDN). Once this standard becomes the international norm, users will be able to receive voice, text, data, and visual information over one standard communications link.

In another example, the Americans, Europeans, and Japanese are racing against each other to develop the technology for high-definition television. The first group to market its technology successfully will have a definite advantage, while the others may well have to conform to their standards.

In the computer industry, some companies are content to share their new technology with partners through strategic alliances, because the more industry players who become involved in your technology, the more likely it will be to gain wide acceptance. Moreover, partners can build on the technology, improve its performance, adapt it for new applications and markets, and increase its chance of wide acceptance.

CHAPTER 3

IS A STRATEGIC ALLIANCE RIGHT FOR YOU?

- **TO PARTNER OR NOT TO PARTNER**
- **ASSESSING YOUR CAPABILITIES**
- **PROTECTING CORE STRENGTHS**
- **SELECTING AN ALLIANCE**
- **COMBINING THE OPTIONS**

"He who has a thorough knowledge of his own conditions as well as of the conditions of the enemy is sure to win in all battles."

"He who has a thorough knowledge of his own conditions but not the conditions of the enemy has an even chance of winning and losing a battle."

"He who has neither a thorough knowledge of his own conditions nor of the enemy's is sure to lose in every battle."

Sun Tzu, The Art of War *(New York: Oxford University Press).*

When and Why to Partner

Forming a strategic alliance requires a good deal of careful preparation. It demands a thorough understanding of your situation, your options, and your potential partners. The better prepared you are, the more likely it is that your alliance will succeed.

In itself, an alliance cannot give your company a strategic direction. Instead, the decision to engage in a partnership should be part of an overall corporate strategy. Rushing into an alliance in the hope that a synergistic plan will somehow evolve is not good business sense. Too many firms underestimate the amount of work that is involved in establishing a successful alliance.

Do you really need a partner? Selecting a partner and managing an alliance take a lot of time and effort. The first step is to determine precisely what you need to defend or enhance your competitive position—to find out what you need, rather than what you want.

The decision to enter into an alliance should be based on an accurate and dispassionate evaluation of the skills and resources that your firm needs to meet its competitive objectives. Which of these skills and resources does your firm already possess? What further ones are needed? The answers to these questions will help you determine whether it is best to go it alone or form an alliance.

A SWOT analysis—a four-column matrix in which you list your firm's Strengths, Weaknesses, Opportunities and the Threats facing it—is commonly used for this kind of assessment. Using a SWOT analysis you can:

- identify the factors that have contributed to the past and present success of the business;

- provide an inventory of the company's skills and resources;

- pinpoint the business strengths that can be used as the foundations for future strategy and identify the serious weaknesses;

- identify the key areas where you are stronger or weaker than your major rivals.

Appendix A, *A Strategic Audit*, contains worksheets that will help you determine the current status of each aspect of your business.

Why Xerox Prefers Strategic Alliances

When expanding into new product markets, Xerox of the United States strongly prefers strategic alliances to acquisitions. Xerox managers find that strategic alliances are more flexible, allowing them to withdraw from a project if it is not achieving desired results. Also, they discovered that many highly qualified personnel left the companies Xerox acquired, taking valuable skills with them. Xerox has had considerable success with its corporate alliances in Europe and in Asia (Rank Xerox and Fuji Xerox).

Diagram 7   Overall Corporate Strategy

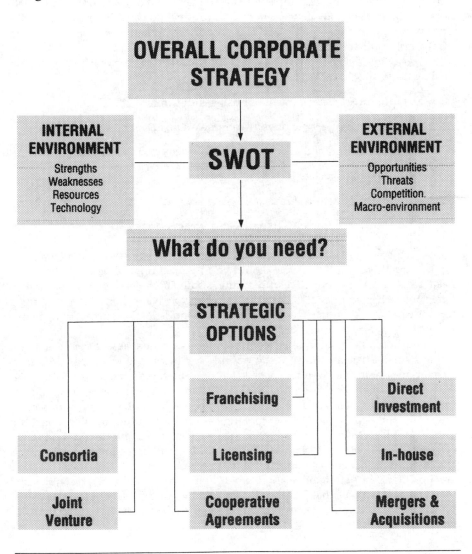

Assessing Your Capabilities

Defining your goals requires an examination of your present situation. Using a SWOT analysis, you can determine the present position of your firm in each of its business segments. Then you can decide where you would like to be and how you are going to get there.

The competitiveness of your products or services will depend on such issues as technology, competitor intensity, cost, quality, and the ability to develop appropriate market niches. You will want to consider your strengths and weaknesses in marketing, new development, and production capabilities. The issues of diversification and integration are also important. What new forms of opportunity and competition exist in your industry?

The analysis will allow you to identify specific gaps or weaknesses in your business, and should include:

- a competitive assessment of business dynamics;

- a technology review of your company's position in the industry;

- an evaluation of market segmentation, size, and growth rate;

- product life cycles;

- opportunities and threats; and

- an audit of company strengths and weaknesses.

Once you have examined your strengths and weaknesses in the context of your competitive objectives, you should be in a position to determine what you need to obtain these objectives. In facing strategic choices, it is important to determine what you need as opposed to what you want. For example, do you need greater distribution capacity, access to technological resources, new financing, or foreign market presence?

Once you have determined your competitive needs, assess the options for filling them. What are the strategic options for moving the company from its current position to the desirable one? What does each option entail?

If the difference can be met through in-house efforts within a reasonable time frame, then a strategic alliance is unnecessary. If the obstacle is simply financial, then you might consider looking for investors rather than partners. But if there is still something missing, such as special expertise, product development synergy, or market presence, then examine strategic alliances more closely.

One of the benefits of going through this exercise is that it clarifies what you are looking for in a strategic relationship. It helps you to define the resources and the type of company that will be needed in the alliance. It gives you a better picture of the skills and resources that the ideal partner must have to make your venture successful.

Protecting Core Strengths

In deciding whether to enter into a strategic alliance, it is important to ensure you are not inadvertently creating a competitor, or giving away competitive advantage. Extreme caution should be exercised in seeking alliance partners, and throughout the negotiation process, in order to protect your market share and core strengths.

A company's core strengths can be defined as the qualities that make it unique and valuable in the marketplace and that separate it from its competitors. Any alliance that threatens a company's core strengths is a bad alliance, for the resulting loss of uniqueness invariably leads to a corresponding loss of market share.

Companies contemplating entering into strategic alliances should have a good understanding of what their core strengths are, and seek partners with little motive or ability to compromise them. If the potential exists for an alliance partner to gain control over your core strengths, precautions must be taken in negotiating and structuring the alliance agreement to minimize this danger.

Similarly, alliances that preserve a company's core strengths, but result in a partner developing similar strengths, should be avoided. The resulting homogenization of skills could end up diluting your firm's competitive advantage.

Careful thought should go into determining what your core strengths are. Often, the answers are less obvious than they first appear.

For example, core strengths do not always correspond to a company's major area of expenditure. In the airline industry, the bulk of each carrier's capital is tied up in its fleet. But planes vary little from airline to airline, the maintenance and baggage handling is often contracted out, and bookings are handled by alliances with other carriers. The core strength of any one company lies in its management know-how—including scheduling, labor relations, service quality, marketing, and airport access.[1]

Identifying core strengths comes down to determining what qualities give a company its advantage in the marketplace. Core strengths can include such things as product quality, image or price, market access, operating strengths, technological know-how, organization, and finance. Precautions companies can take to protect their core strengths include:

- ensuring quality is maintained when licensing products, to preserve brand-name integrity;

---

[1]   Jordan D. Lewis, *Partnerships for Profit* (New York: Free Press, 1990).

- maintaining value-adding strength in design, manufacturing, or related services to keep a manufacturing partner from entering the market on its own;

- safeguarding critical technological know-how from alliance partners;

- limiting market access through specific clauses in alliance agreements;

- barring access to all human resources, technology, information, and facilities outside the scope of the alliance; and

- limiting the scope of an alliance until proof of success can be tested.

Selecting a Strategic Alliance

If you decide the cooperative route is right for you, the next step is to consider the various kinds of strategic alliances. Analyze the pros and cons of each type in the context of your needs and objectives.

Be sure that your objectives have been defined clearly. If you enter an alliance without a clear set of objectives, you risk an eventual loss of control, allowing your partner's needs to dictate the direction of your alliance. This problem becomes particularly evident later on, when the alliance must choose between opportunities that favor very different strategies. Each partner's set of objectives should complement the other's, and both sets should fit into an overall strategy. Otherwise, the alliance will be lopsided and may not meet your needs.

Benetton's Integrated Infrastructure

Benetton, the Italian clothing manufacturer, has woven a computer-linked network that has greatly increased its performance. It sells all of its garments through stores with which it has an exclusive franchising arrangement. Each store is linked to the manufacturers by computer. The garments are not made until they have been ordered by one of the stores, minimizing warehousing requirements, and enhancing Benetton's sensitivity and responsiveness to market changes.

Benetton has subcontracted out about 80 percent of its labor-intensive production activities, but it maintains responsibility for quality control for capital-intensive functions.

Consider how various types of alliances may affect your core business. Many companies maintain close control of their core business and form partnerships solely in noncore areas. Firms deciding to enter partnerships should be aware that alliances can lead to dependence on outside firms, or the transference of expertise to competitors.

Once you have decided what type of strategic alliance is best for you, the next step involves searching for a suitable partner. Be sure you are ready and willing to take on the large commitment involved in finding the right partner, structuring the deal, and managing the venture. Alliances can succeed only if partners are willing and able to commit enough time, energy, resources, financing, and skilled people to make them work.

Traditional Strategies

In-house development allows for a high degree of control. This strategy worked well when corporations were growing quickly, diversifying themselves across markets and opportunities—and it works well today in mature industries.

Direct investment can take two forms. Forming a wholly-owned subsidiary can be a very effective way to adapt to a local market. The high degree of control the parent company retains is particularly useful for complex products or services. And the risk of losing secrets to competitors is minimized.

The drawback is that the head office may limit the ability of its subsidiaries to respond quickly and flexibly to changes in local markets.

The second form involves the purchase of an equity share in another company. If the share is large enough, an investor can influence the direction of the company through positions on the board.

But simply injecting financing into a company is often not enough. Today, investment with real clout is investment accompanied by real expertise.

Mergers and acquisitions allow a firm to maintain control over a project. Since there is no need to cooperate with outsiders, your firm's knowledge stays in-house, and management can more effectively monitor and coordinate divisions within the firm.

The problem with mergers and acquisitions is that they are slow and cumbersome. They raise overhead dramatically. They often involve extensive renovations. And a corporate culture clash may develop.

Combining the Options

Just as a financial analyst builds a portfolio of stocks, a firm can build a portfolio of strategic alliances. By sharing the initial investment in each venture with allies, a company frees up resources. This allows it to enter other areas of opportunity.

Putting It All Together

- Know your objectives

- Get all the facts

- Identify your opportunities

- Determine your needs

- Build on your strengths

- Know your competitors

- Understand the market

- Evaluate your options

Thus the firm is able to avoid overextending itself. It diversifies by leveraging its strengths, rather than by straying from its area of excellence.

In an important sense, this is an investment portfolio—what is new is that expertise is often the crucial part of the investment. Companies that collect portfolios of strategic alliances are giving rise to a new type of corporation that is less monolithic. Each forms a network of business organizations, ranging from divisions of the original company, to wholly-owned subsidiaries, to discrete joint ventures.

In these companies, the head office creates and manages the formal linkages of its network and sets the overall priorities. Because more responsibilities have been delegated, the individual parts of the network are able to respond quickly and flexibly to their own markets.

It may well be that in the future most firms will belong to teams of companies that compete with one another. No doubt, the ties between companies throughout the business community will be as complex as the technologies that support them.

Corning's Global Network

Corning Inc. entered into its first joint venture—to make cartons for glass products—in 1924. By 1989, it had 15 ventures involving 11 partners around the world, and joint ventures accounted for about half of its income.

"The successful operation of a global management network requires a new mind-set," says chairman James Houghton. "A network is egalitarian. There is no parent company. A corporate staff is no more, or less, important than a line organization group. And being a part of a joint venture is just as important as working at the hub of the network."

The major job of the head office is providing the information, resources, and guidance needed to keep the network functioning. Corning's network ranges from traditional line divisions to wholly owned subsidiaries and joint ventures. Corning's joint ventures range from a 40-year-old alliance with Dow Chemicals to one set up a year and a half ago with IBM. Corning has ventures with Siemens, the West German engineering corporation, and with Samsung, the South Korean consumer electronics corporation. Corning has six joint ventures in optical fibers throughout Europe and Asia. Each joint venture makes a unique contribution to Corning's strategic position. For example, through its partnership with Ciba-Geigy of Switzerland, Corning gained access to improved technology for manufacturing medical diagnostic equipment. Through Asahi Video Products, Corning gained access to new technology for making TV picture tubes and access to the U.S. market—a market that has been dominated by the Japanese. Asahi Glass in return gained access to Corning's plants in the U.S. and in Mexico.

Source: Fortune, *March 27, 1989.*

Diagram 8   A New Type of Corporation

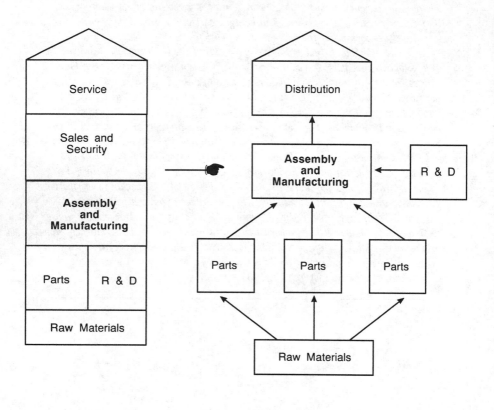

CHAPTER 4

FINDING THE RIGHT PARTNER

- ## PARTNERS ARE CORNERSTONES
- ## KEYS TO PARTNERING

The Vital Partnership

Partners are the cornerstones of any successful alliance structure. Your partner must have the skills and resources you are seeking, and you need to be able to work closely together. Without trust and without the right chemistry, partners are unable to achieve the cooperation necessary for successful alliances.

It is vital that you find the right partner. Make sure you carry out a thorough search. The right partner cannot guarantee success, but an alliance with the wrong partner will almost certainly fail to achieve your strategic objectives. One of the key reasons cited by experienced managers for poor performance or unsuccessful partnerships is bad partner selection. And, as many firms have found out, the choice of an inappropriate or inadequate partner can have serious long-term competitive and financial implications.

Creating a strategic alliance is a time-consuming and expensive process. Developing criteria, selecting a partner, and negotiating an agreement can take from 100 to 5,000 hours. Nevertheless, taking the time to do a thorough partner search is an investment that will likely prove critical to the long-term success of your venture.

The process needs to be approached with considerable patience and with realistic expectations. And remember, the selection process can become even more complex for international alliances. A company unwilling to accept these costs should probably consider other investment options.

An Ideal Blend of Partners

Harris Corp. of the United States achieved an ideal blend of partners to manufacture satellite networks. Harris looked to Matsushita Electric to provide radio-frequency terminals for the network. In return, it signed a cross-distribution agreement with the Japanese firm to let Matsushita distribute the network in Asia.

In addition, Harris gave Philips NV of the Netherlands the right to distribute the network in Western Europe in exchange for a supply of input-output processors.

Finally, by forming an alliance with AT&T to provide a new Ku-band satellite business communications service, Harris gained technology as well as enhancing its ability to penetrate the lucrative U.S. market.

Surprisingly, many managers do not spend enough time exploring the issue of compatibility between their own firms and prospective partner companies. Yet finding a compatible partner is not simply a matter of finding one with complementary skills. It is also vital that your organizations and your strategies complement each other.

Clearly, the first step in a partner search is to identify firms that possess the resources and capabilities that you lack, but that are necessary for achieving your strategic objectives. Complementary technology is the minimum criterion for selecting a partner. The next step is to make sure that you can cooperate easily and effectively with your potential partner. Otherwise, you are likely to experience substantial coordination and communications costs as well as a high level of frustration.

The extent and nature of your need to interact with your partner will be based on a number of factors, including uncertainty in markets, technology, and resource supply, as well as the complexity of the tasks involved. The more you need to interact with your partner, the more important it is to find a partner whose organization complements your own.

You will need to consider questions of size, organizational structure, management style, operating policies, philosophy, etc. There are numerous examples of organizational clashes or culture shock between businesses that had appeared to be compatible. Take the time to find out if you can really work with a potential partner.

It is also important to understand what potential partners want from your relationship. Are the goals of your firms compatible? The more divergence there is between your own and your partner's objectives, the greater the risk of dissatisfaction and associated problems.

Structuring Complementary Alliances

The demand for new and innovative window-forming technology to complement increasingly aerodynamic car designs has led Ford into a minority investment alliance with Excel Industries, a leading glass manufacturer. Because window and auto body designs must complement each other precisely, alliance projects call for close cooperation between the companies for extended periods of time. And yet the structure of the alliance is such that mammoth Ford does not dominate or inhibit the flexibility of its much smaller partner.

While Ford owns a substantial block of Excel stock, and Ford members sit on the Excel board of directors, the glass-forming company retains a great deal of autonomy. Ford's rights as an investor are restricted to policy measures that bolster its partner's strength. Ford puts no constraints on Excel's financial matters, and has no access to Excel's business data. Ford is perfectly happy in this relationship, knowing that Excel's independence is part of its strength.[1]

In the last analysis, the overriding consideration must be the potential partner's commitment and trustworthiness. Trust is crucial, especially where areas of core competence are involved. Today's partner might be tomorrow's competitor. Exposing your strategy or technology to an unreliable partner could seriously erode your competitive advantage.

The effort involved in identifying the right partner will likely repay you many times. It can mean the avoidance of delays, misunderstandings, and the breakup of your alliance due to unsatisfactory performance. In the end, there is no substitute for the intensive screening of partners. If you are unable to find a

---

1   Jordan D. Lewis, *Partnerships for Profit* (New York: Free Press, 1990), p. 116.

partner who is compatible and trustworthy, you would probably be better off looking for an alternative way of achieving your objectives.

Remember, in any successful partnership, regardless of the structure of the deal, the whole will be greater than the sum of the parts. Each partner will use the other's resources to maximize its own strengths. Together the partners can create and bring to market new technologies, products, and services that neither might have been able to create on its own.

U.S. Memories

If an alliance is to succeed, partners must be prepared to commit sufficient resources. According to the leaders of U.S. Memories, it was this failure that led to the downfall of the proposed manufacturer of memory chips. U.S. Memories was formed at the request of U.S. computer companies to create additional U.S. sources of memory chips, reducing the American dependency on Japanese suppliers. At the time of the start-up, American computer companies were experiencing a shortage of the chips.

U.S. Memories was looking for investments from U.S. electronics and semiconductor companies for its $1 billion memory chip plant. In the second half of 1989, chip supplies increased and prices fell, and as the chip shortage crisis waned, so did the interest of American industry.

"They made tactical rather than strategic decisions. There is no shortage of dynamic random-access memory (d-ram) chips today, and they are not thinking about tomorrow," said Wilfred Corrigan, chairman of LSI Logic and chairman of U.S. Memories.

"In the U.S., we have an all-star computer industry team, whereas the Japanese are team players. Teamwork will always triumph in the end," says the president of U.S. Memories, Mr. Sanford Kane.

Source: Financial Times, January 17, 1990.

Keys to Successful Partnering:

- Be willing to commit time and resources to the analysis and selection of partners;

- Identify clearly and precisely the specific venture to be pursued and what is expected from your partner—and make this known to prospective partners;

- Maintain frank and open communications with your partner;

- Don't be misled by superficial similarities between you and your potential partner;

- Look at the potential partner's balance sheet, financial stability, plans for growth, and profit orientation;

- If the partner is an unknown to you, start small;

- Start negotiating at the top with the most senior person in the company.

Capability

Assess the competitive strengths and weaknesses of your partner and discuss any particular areas of concern frankly and openly. It may be wise to develop a pre-incorporation agreement identifying the various strengths of the respective partners and what each will contribute.

In areas where technological obsolescence is rapid, be cautious about making assumptions about the capability of a potential partner. Ensure that you have sufficient bargaining leverage to reduce the risk of your partner demanding far more than it gives to the venture.

Objectives

A forthright and candid discussion of broad strategic objectives is essential. Be sure you know the real reason why the potential partner wants to participate.

Some Attributes of a Good Partnership:

- Complementary technical skills and resources

- Mutual need

- Financial capability

- Complementary size

- A compatible view of strategy and objectives

- Complementary operating policies

- Compatible management teams

- Mutual trust and commitment

- Low risk of becoming a competitor

Determine how critical the proposed venture is to your partner's long-term business strategy. Does your partner need the venture to meet its own tactical and strategic objectives?

Don't assume that your objectives are the same. Ensure that time horizons are mutually acceptable and expected returns are clearly understood. Determine whether the potential partner is in direct competition with you and, if so, in which markets.

Chemistry

Pay careful attention to chemistry and organizational fit. Are your business cultures and attitudes compatible? Examine your potential partner's orientation toward risk and profit, as well as its staff and style of management. Research its track record on cooperation.

Major cultural differences between partners may prove to be obstacles. Assess the cultural and organizational fit as early in the discussions as possible.

Protection

Make sure there are measures in place to protect your contribution (e.g., proprietary technology). In the case of a foreign partner, ensure that you know the intellectual property laws in force in its country. Take measures to guard against unfair appropriation of your know-how.

Increasingly, the sort of technology at risk in an alliance cannot be protected by patents. This is especially true in young, dynamic fields such as biotechnology. To the extent that your alliance involves new patentable property, find the appropriate legal protection for these rights before getting too deeply into the negotiations.

Overseas

If you are contemplating an alliance in a foreign country, talk to people who have had partnering experience there. Get to know the intellectual-property and trade-secret laws in your partner's jurisdiction.

Know the various legal risks regarding competition in the market you are entering. Don't be deceived by the easy joint-venture meetings at trade shows, etc.

Irrevocable Differences

North American firms seeking joint ventures in Europe need to pay careful attention to differences in corporate culture and philosophy. Cascades Inc. discovered that different operating philosophies can create irrevocable problems between partners. In mid-1987, the Quebec firm formed a joint venture with Groupe Pinault SA of France. Each parent controlled 50 percent of the resulting company, La Société Franco-Canadienne des Papiers.

The purpose of the joint venture was to take over and operate Chapelle Darblay SA, a failing French newsprint company located near Rouen. La Société bought an 85 percent share in Chapelle Darblay, with Credit Lyonnais SA holding the remainder.

Cascades was responsible for operating Chapelle Darblay, while Groupe Pinault supplied the raw materials. In 1988, Cascades discovered that it actually did not know its partner as well as it thought it did. The two firms fell out with each other because of their different management approaches. Eventually, they took their differences to a French commercial tribunal—with both partners seeking control of the venture. Part of the reason the tribunal found in favor of Groupe Pinault was that the French government had given Chapelle Darblay a total of $300 million both before and after La Société Franco-Canadienne had bought it. The tribunal also ruled that Cascades be given $5.9 million as compensation for its management services.

Cascades sold its share in the venture for $2.8 million soon after the decision. Today, Cascades is not bitter about the loss, but rather views the affair as an important learning experience.

There are several places to turn for assistance in gathering information and new market ideas. Start with a list of companies with real potential for international partnerships and growth. Make this list available to community developers, business associations, and government agencies in target regions. Ask them to suggest the names of companies in their region that complement the capabilities of your company. Then organize meetings at which your company can meet with potential partners.

Some regions around the world have databases that contain useful information. Search for regions that offer a good "fit" for your company. There are also numerous databases that are geared to small and medium enterprises.

Effective partnering depends on effective networking. This is especially true for smaller businesses. Formal and informal linkages are important ways of developing contacts, securing business information, initiating cooperative activities, accessing new sources of capital, and obtaining technology.

Remember, you are not alone. Many governments provide useful assistance. In the United States, the Commerce Department's U.S. and Foreign Commercial Service provides companies with detailed advice, business contacts, and direct access to over 95 percent of the world market for U.S. products. Each state also has a department of industrial development that maintains useful databases on its region.

In Canada both the federal and provincial governments provide useful information, resources, and networks. Provincial governments have staff working in the field with companies. Agencies focusing on local development (for instance, provincial ministries, the Atlantic Canada Opportunities Agency, Industry Science and Technology Canada, the Western Diversification Office) operate networks of regional offices.

There are other networks available to you as well. Associations of industrial developers can serve as focal points for the exchange of information. And science parks (centers formed for scientific research) have formed an international organization designed to compare strategies and devise ways of complementing each other's initiatives.

Explore opportunities for using consultants and specialists to scout potential partnerships and to set up new networks. And keep in mind that some venture companies with investments in a group of local firms may seek partnerships with companies that have invested in a complementary group of firms, as a means of helping their clients expand and develop.

Sources of Expertise on Strategic Alliance Partnering:

- Private consultants

- State/provincial programs

- Databases

- Industrial developers' associations

- Personal networks

- International associations

- Intermediaries

- Federal programs

CHAPTER 5

NEGOTIATING A STRATEGIC ALLIANCE

- **NEGOTIATIONS SET THE TONE**
- **WARNING SIGNS**
- **BUSINESS AND LEGAL FRAMEWORKS**
- **MARKETING ISSUES**
- **LEGAL AND TECHNOLOGY ISSUES**
- **EXIT CLAUSES**

Setting the Tone

In an important sense, negotiations between partners lie at the heart of the whole strategic alliance process. Your negotiations with your partner will set the tone and create the structure of your relationship.

It is important that the communication be honest and frank. Cooperation depends on an atmosphere of mutual respect and trust. But trust does not mean ignoring difficult questions or brushing aside serious reservations. Trust allows partners to meet challenges and solve problems together.

Nor does trust mean ignoring real security issues. Frank and clear definitions of intent, of the scope of cooperation, and of the terms of confidentiality are important. The avoidance of important and legitimate concerns can only lead to confusion, unease, and suspicion.

In many successful strategic alliances, the negotiations never actually come to an end. While it is important to structure your alliance so that it will be able to face every challenge you and your partners can anticipate, it is unlikely you will anticipate every new development that will occur. After all, alliances are designed to succeed in rapidly changing environments.

Objectives, resources, and the relative power of parent companies change. Markets shift, new technologies emerge, and customers' needs evolve. Because no company can anticipate all these variables, it is impossible to take into account every possible contingency in drafting an alliance agreement.

The flexibility to evolve is one of the benchmarks of a successful alliance. A study of 150 strategic alliances undertaken by McKinsey & Company analysts found that 67 percent ran into trouble in the first two years. Those with the flexibility to evolve were better able to recover. In addition, the success rate of alliances that expanded the scope of their charters over time was more than twice that of companies whose charters remained unchanged.[1]

You can build flexibility into the structure of your agreement by specifying areas to be renegotiated in the event of a change. The proposed changes or specifications must be mutually acceptable, or else the changes will not be an improvement. You will also want to leave open details that cannot yet be specified because they are dependent on tasks that will be completed in the future. Agreeing to determine the details at a more appropriate time saves time and builds trust by establishing intent.

It is not enough to structure an alliance so that it is flexible. Partners themselves need to be flexible and open to renegotiating their agreement as vital circumstances change.

Take, for example, two companies that have allied with each other in order to share their respective strengths in technology and distribution. Prices often decrease as products age, and if the partner who is responsible for technology refuses to renegotiate its royalty payments, the distribution partner could wind up losing money in sales.

In another case, a new competitor might take the market by storm, forcing your alliance to redevelop a portion of its product to maintain market share. New industry-wide standards or new government regulations may also cause drastic market changes that require immediate and cooperative response.

---

1   Joel Bleeke and David Ernst, "The Way to Win in Cross-Border Alliances," *Harvard Business Review*, November-December 1991, p. 127.

For Better Strategic Alliances:

- Devise tests to verify that you really need a strategic alliance.

- Prepare your own people for strategic alliances.

- Take care to choose the right partner.

- Explicitly accommodate the dynamics of your strategic alliance relationship in your written agreement.

- Institute a formal review process.

- Encourage the formal sharing of alliance knowledge and experience.

- Appoint a formal champion for strategic alliances.

Questions to Consider When Structuring a Joint Venture

Because joint ventures lead more autonomous lives than other forms of strategic alliances, prospective partners need to consider a whole new range of issues concerning the operation and governance of their joint venture:

- *How will the management and board of directors of the joint venture be chosen?*

- *Will the joint venture rely on its own staff or on service contracts from the partners for financial, management, or technical services?*

- *What happens if the joint venture needs additional capital?*

- *How will the joint venture decide whether to expand into new businesses?*

- *What will happen if one of the partners wants to sell his interest in the venture?*

- *How will a decision to liquidate the joint venture be made?*

- *How will ownership of the joint venture's technology and other assets be divided if the venture is liquidated?*

The members of your negotiating team should be drawn from a variety of areas and management levels, ensuring that the team has a command of all the issues affecting your strategic alliance—from broad strategic concerns to legal and technical details. And it is important that your team does its homework, studying your partner's firm and your own firm, as well as material relating specifically to the strategic alliance.

It is vital that team members have the sensitivity and confidence to be able to bridge cultural gaps. Where partners speak different languages, make sure that you have the means to make sophisticated translations. If your communication is limited to simple words or inadequate translations, subtle misunderstandings can easily become major obstructions.

Some involvement by top management is important. Their presence signals real commitment on the part of the firm, helping to bring both the partner and your own employees onside. Senior executives have the broad strategic understanding and the clout that can help to keep talks on track and that can break deadlocks in negotiation.

It is, however, usually a good idea to limit the involvement of parent executives. At a certain point, personnel with a better grasp of technical, operational, and legal details should take over negotiations. Senior executives have been known to avoid raising thorny questions in order to maintain a pleasant, collegial atmosphere. They may also lack detailed familiarity with issues that are the province of lower levels of management and assume that difficult details will be ironed out later.

Some firms believe negotiating teams should include people who will actually be involved in the managing of the alliance. It is an opportunity for them to get to know their future colleagues and to help shape and fully understand the structure of the alliance.

Other firms have found that such staff are better introduced later in the negotiating process, after the controversial issues have been hammered out. This saves them from becoming caught between the interest of the parent firm and their desire to nurture a harmonious working relationship with their opposites.

Every alliance needs a champion. You should appoint at least one person with enough clout to make things happen. The champion becomes the key catalyst for the alliance within your firm. He or she is the driving force, taking responsibility within your firm for its creation and often serving as the chief negotiator.

The ongoing commitment of a champion within each partner firm is essential to the establishment of a successful alliance. For this reason, it is a good idea to have as many as three champions. Then, if a champion leaves the firm, the formation of the alliance is only slowed, rather than derailed.

The members of the negotiating team should meet at least once before entering negotiations. This gives them a chance to get to know each other, to assign roles, and to set goals, strategies, and tactics. Not only will this increase their effectiveness as a team, it also ensures that they do not send confusing signals to their opposite numbers.

What Are the Warning Signals?

In negotiations, pay careful attention to the attitudes and behavior of your potential partners. If you get the sense that something is not quite right, take the feeling seriously. Watch out for these warning signals, which indicate that you might be entering a venture with a high risk of failure:

- You experience difficulty agreeing on what are proprietary data.

- Your potential partner is trying to push you into making quick commitments.

- You sense they are not being honest and straightforward with you.

- They are uncomfortable discussing their intentions and plans.

- They are spending a lot of money without serious thought.

Technology Bytes for Market Bites

Two arch rivals discovered they had interests that complemented each other. Toshiba wanted to gain access to Motorola's microprocessor technology. And Motorola wanted a piece of the Japanese market. They decided on a swap: access to technology in exchange for market access.

But Motorola was wary of giving away its technology without a guarantee that its competitor would follow through on its promise. The result was a step-by-step exchange. For each step Toshiba takes to carry out its promise to help Motorola enter the rich but notoriously inhospitable Japanese market, Motorola will give the Japanese company part of its logic-chip technology.

Establishing Business and Legal Frameworks

Negotiating an alliance agreement involves reaching an understanding on a general level, and then on a more detailed, formal level. These two stages of the agreement are known as the business framework and the legal framework, respectively.

Once the teams from each firm have met and gained some familiarity with each other, the first item on the agenda is the construction of the business

---

Constructing the Strategic Alliance

1. Building the business framework
2. The MOU and exchange of contract language.
3. Building the legal framework

---

framework. The two teams try to reach an agreement that clearly defines the objectives of the alliance and—in general terms—the form the alliance should take to best meet these objectives. If you know what you have, what you want, and what success means, the business framework for your deal should be relatively clear.

But do not be surprised if this part of the negotiations takes longer than you expected. Taking the time to ensure that both you and your partner share clearly defined objectives, and that your business ideas are sound, will be invaluable when you come to fill in the details of the legal framework.

Once both teams have come to a shared understanding of the business framework, they express their agreement in a memorandum of understanding (MOU).

The MOU provides a basis for the more detailed and formal negotiations of the legal framework. The length of the MOU depends on the individual situation: it can consist of a single paragraph, or it can be as much as ten or more pages. MOUs are important for several reasons:

- they help to introduce clarity early in negotiations;

- they can be used to define confidentiality, lessening the risk of loss of proprietary information during negotiations; and

- they provide an opportunity for the partners to agree not to enter into negotiations with other firms.

The teams also begin to exchange contract language, setting the stage for the construction of the legal framework. An important consideration when building the business framework is how internal politics within both firms will affect the deal. If there are winners and losers within the firms, be prepared for conflict. This is especially true when small firms form alliances with large firms.

A common obstacle in large firms is the "not invented here" syndrome: employees resenting what they view as outside interference when outside firms are included, through alliances, in traditionally in-house operations. When this takes place, the commitment vital to the success of the alliance is jeopardized. For this reason, you should consider what incentives will be needed to ensure the commitment of key people.

The Dramatic Saab-GM Story

Saab is one of the smallest car manufacturing operations in the world. It's products are sold at the upper end of the market—making it attractive to the swelling ranks of high-income baby boomers. Nonetheless, in 1988 Saab found itself in trouble, and it was looking for a partner to rescue its car operations without taking all control away from Saab.

Saab and GM concluded an aerospace deal in June 1989. As a courtesy, Georg Karnsund, the chief executive officer for Saab-Scandia told the GM chairman Roger Smith that Saab was in major negotiations with Ford concerning Saab's car-making operations. Karnsund offered Smith a deal. The offer was declined because at that time GM wanted to stay focused on a deal it was trying to negotiate with Jaguar. Then in November, GM lost the Jaguar deal to Ford.

By that time, Ford had dropped out of its talks, leaving Saab with little choice but to enter negotiations with Fiat. Fiat was very confident that the deal would close, but Saab was not happy. Fiat was dictating terms, was not interested in a wide-ranging deal, and intended to replace the management leaders of the Saab car division.

On November 14, Robert Eaton, president of GM Europe (and now chairman of Chrysler), phoned Karnsund, and invited him to GM's European headquarters in Zurich to examine a partnership. They met the next week and agreed to set up a small strategy team of project planners and marketing people to see if an alliance would work. Within three days, the team produced an outline of the product program. Within six days, Eaton was leading a GM team on a tour of all of Saab's operations in Sweden and Finland. During the course of the negotiations and during this tour there was a mounting sense of shared enthusiasm and confidence, a positive chemistry reinforced by complementary goals and by a history of previous alliances in other areas.

Karnsund and the GM leaders unveiled the agreement at a Saab board meeting at 9 a.m., December 15, 1989. At 10 a.m., shocked Fiat leaders were informed of the Saab-GM deal.

Source: Financial Times, *December 22, 1989.*

The legal framework is the actual working out of the general terms agreed upon in the business framework. The legal framework establishes the alliance structure and methods of capitalization and control. It defines the rights and responsibilities of each partner regarding the use and support of technology, licensing, and marketing.

Legal topics to be addressed vary depending on the individual agreement. The legal framework should be sufficient to protect the business objectives and competitive positions of both sides.

At the outset, the areas of control and responsibility should be identified. In a joint venture, there are either majority and minority shareholders or the ownership is divided equally. While the division of ownership affects the degree of operational control exercised, the relationship between ownership and control is by no means fixed.

Some partners view a 50-50 split as a symbol of equality and of the commitment and continuing interest of both partners in the joint venture. On the other hand, partners with a majority equity position usually exercise a greater degree of control over the venture. Nevertheless, they will not be able to dictate everything.

Minority partners can influence areas such as human resources and the appointment of managers. They can also safeguard their position by establishing their right to veto decisions made by the majority partner regarding key staff appointments, major financial expenditures, major changes in business strategy, or shareholdings.

Occasionally, joint venture partners who hold less than 25 percent of the equity are considered to be only investors, with minimal responsibilities.

Some Important Marketing Issues

The control and coordination of the marketing plan can be difficult when both partners market the product or line of products. Key issues to address are:

- Who decides what the product will be?

- Who designs the product?

- Who chooses the product name?

- Will you share advertising or marketing campaigns?

- Who decides on improvements or new additions to the product line?

- Who is responsible for warranty obligations?

- Who is responsible if a customer is injured (product liability)?

- What happens if the product infringes on the intellectual property rights of someone else?

- What happens to marketing rights if the partnership ends?

Key Technology Issues

Partners need to resolve:

- Questions of ownership of technologies developed by the alliance.

- The right to use and market:
  1. technologies to be developed
  2. technologies from outside sources
  3. core technologies

- Division of royalties if a partner markets technology—or products based on technology—developed by the alliance.

- Ownership and rights to use improvements in the technology.

- Decision-making procedures concerning products based on new technology.

- Legal rights involved if a third party infringes on technology developed by the partnership.

Control of a Joint Venture

There are four major ways of defining the control of a joint venture:

1. Dominant partner: one partner dominates the decision-making process. This one is relatively easily to manage.

2. Shared management: each partner plays an active role in operational or strategic decisions. Joint ventures with shared management are more likely to experience conflict, but because both partners have a voice and a hand in the venture, there is also more opportunity for both sides to be heard and effective compromises reached.

3. Split control: each partner controls specified areas. Hopefully, partners are assigned areas of responsibility that are close to their strategic objectives. Because neither partner enjoys decisive control of the venture, the coordination and maintenance of clear objectives is extremely important.

4. Independent: the joint venture's general manager takes responsibility for decisions. The autonomy of the joint venture must be recognized and respected by all of the partners.

Responsibility means cost. Whoever controls the alliance must have the resources and the will to take on the attendant responsibilities. Exercising control over the management of a joint venture, for example, will divert attention from other activities in the parent company, and may result in increased overhead and human resources costs.

When constructing the legal framework, it is especially important to make sure that the agreement defines both the scope of cooperation and the procedures involved. This will facilitate the smooth functioning of the venture, and it will also protect the relationship by reducing the likelihood that trade secrets or technology will stray to competitors.

For example, in a joint R&D effort, the creation of a separate entity (joint venture) to perform the work ensures that the technological contributions of each partner can be owned by all participants. If structured accordingly, future spin-offs or future-generation products from the venture will also be jointly owned. This precaution ensures that proprietary technology shared in one alliance does not stray to a different alliance.

Some multinational firms point out that mutual dependence can be fostered with many informal linkages between partners, and the greater the reciprocal needs from each other's markets, technology, and capital, the less likely it is that one partner will betray the other.

Partners Can Be Competitors

Partners can also be potential competitors, and you should take care to safeguard your future market share. When Toshiba entered into a joint venture with Westinghouse to manufacture picture tubes, it needed to find a way to safeguard its advanced technology for color picture tubes. Toshiba restricted the venture's licensing arrangement to a specific type of tubes. The joint venture cannot manufacture other tubes that belong to Toshiba without Toshiba's permission.

Another important way to protect market share is to establish different agreements for different areas of the alliance. Westinghouse used this strategy in its alliance with Mitsubishi by signing separate agreements for sales and for marketing. This way, Westinghouse can guard its extensive distribution network and protect its own market share if it begins to be threatened by the alliance.

Exit Clauses

It is wise to build exit clauses into alliance agreements. Clearly defined responsibilities, rights, and procedures reduce tensions. The partners know what is expected of them and know the consequences of breaking up the alliance without careful consideration. And exit clauses become especially important if a conflict arises that cannot be resolved.

Unfortunately, too many managers do not familiarize themselves with the terms of the legal agreement until they are in dire need of an effective exit clause. Then they can only hope that their lawyers served them well when they defined the terms of the exit clause.

Clearly, management should be aware of the various options and ramifications of each part of the legal agreement as it is being negotiated. When the alliance has ended, it may well be the exit clause that determines your strategic position.

A number of joint ventures terminate with one of the parent companies buying out the other. This typically occurs when the core strengths of the respective parents shift over the course of the alliance.

If, for example, a joint venture results in one parent assimilating the core strengths of its partner, the partner's value in the alliance diminishes. The compromised parent may then be pressured to sell its interest in the joint venture, or risk its former partner entering the market on its own, as a competitor.

If this contingency is not foreseen, or prepared for, the long-term strategic goals of joint venture parents could be seriously jeopardized.

Strategic Alliance Buyout Protection

Studies have shown that Japanese parent companies buy out their joint venture partners in a majority of strategic alliance terminations. This can prove dangerous for Western partners, who often seek powerful Japanese companies to partner with. The Fujitsu-Amdahl joint venture shows that long-term strategy and positioning need not be compromised by strategic alliances with aggressive Japanese companies.

The Japanese-American joint venture was struck in 1972, at which time Fujitsu contributed capital and manufacturing skills, while Amdahl brought expertise in mainframe design and architecture, as well as brand-name recognition and U.S. market access.

Because Fujitsu agreed to limit its equity ownership in the alliance to 49.5 percent through April 1994, Amdahl had a 22-year grace period during which it could devote itself to improving its position in the highly competitive computer industry, without fear of its partner turning into a competitor. With Fujitsu's help, Amdahl has been able to meet the rising costs of R&D in developing new mainframe machines, and has improved its rank among U.S. computer manufacturers from nineteenth in 1980 to thirteenth in 1990.[2]

---

2   Joel Bleeke and David Ernst, "The Way to Win in Cross-Border Alliances," *Harvard Business Review*, November-December 1991, pp. 134, 135.

Most of the legal detail in an exit clause is concerned with the dispositions of assets, staff, technology, and patents when an alliance breaks up. In the case of a joint venture, termination clauses usually either give the right of first refusal to the other partner or they dictate the terms of some kind of shotgun sale.

Usually, a share price is specified in the exit clause—after all, it is easier to be objective and arrive at a fair price when you do not know whether you will be the buyer or seller—but it is also possible to leave this sort of arbitration to a third party.

Exit clauses can be formulated implicitly if for some reason it is not possible to settle on an explicit one. What this means is that instead of explicitly defining a point when the alliance would be ended, the agreement includes provisions for renegotiation of the agreement if specific sales or profit targets have not been met within a certain period of time.

It is also possible to stipulate fines a partner must pay if it breaks an alliance unilaterally. But keep in mind, while complex legal detail is often needed by creditors, overzealous attention to minute detail can kill an alliance before it gets off the ground. Another effective way to protect financial partners is to establish benchmarks for the alliance. The risks to investors can be minimized by dispensing capital in increments, each of which is contingent on the achievement of technological or other milestones by specified dates.

CHAPTER 6

MANAGING YOUR STRATEGIC ALLIANCE

- **SUCCESS THROUGH MANAGEMENT**
- **MOTIVATING**
- **COORDINATION AND COMMUNICATION**
- **CONFLICT RESOLUTION**
- **PERFORMANCE MEASUREMENT**

Success Through Management

Clearly, the success of your strategic alliance will depend on the quality of the people who manage it. Strategic alliances pose special organizational problems, and your staff will need special skills to overcome them. They should be thoroughly competent in their normal managerial or technical roles, and they will also need strong interpersonal skills. This is especially true in the case of the general manager.

Finding the right person to run the strategic alliance—or to look after the liaison points between the partners—is of vital importance. Such people must have enough power within your firm to make things happen, and they must have a good understanding of the cultures and the way things run in both of the parent companies. They need to be active listeners, able to sense the unspoken and hidden dynamics of the other side and find the reasonable compromises.

In the case of joint ventures, the general manager can make or break the alliance. Whether recruited from within the company or from outside, the general manager must be able to understand and balance the needs of both parent companies with the interests of the joint venture itself.

It would be a mistake to hire the general manager from within your own ranks in the hope that he or she will favor the interests of your company over those of your partner's. It is upon such short-sighted motivations that joint ventures founder.

Zero-sum games—games in which for every winner there must be a loser—should be avoided. After all, why should a loser cooperate? It is important that managers in a joint venture be able to work well with the general manager and with each other.

Differences in Management Styles

A study by Andre Laurent, a professor at the French business school IN-SEAD, provides interesting examples of how management styles and expectations can vary from culture to culture. The issue was whether a manager is expected to possess precise answers to questions posed by employees.

- *The American manager is not expected to be an expert in all areas.*

- *The British manager is a proverbial generalist.*

- *The German manager is expected to be an expert.*

- *The Latin manager is expected to have the answer because he is in charge.*

- *The Japanese executive knows his subordinates will not ask him a question unless they are confident he can answer it.*

It is not a question of which is the superior method. What is vital is that the international manager learn to recognize and work with the differences. For instance, instead of feeling constrained by the technical and functional orientation of Germans, a budding international manager from, say Britain, could learn to appreciate and fully utilize the depth of technical competence of his German subordinates.

Source: Financial Times, *February 14, 1990.*

Technical staff will probably have to adapt to new ways of doing things and to a new and evolving culture. And, given the rapidly changing environment most strategic alliances have been created to tackle, the success of your venture may well depend on the quick and effective work of your technical people. They will need to have both strong technical and interpersonal skills.

It is important to have an effective system for staff appraisals. Formal staff assessment procedures will allow you to improve areas of venture performance, determine effective rates of pay, and ensure that important functions are carried out correctly. It is probably best if the performance standards used to judge employees in the parent are not applied to the staff of a joint venture. Because both parent companies have their own strategic objectives in mind, it is likely that they will use different criteria when assessing alliance staff. As long as these differences are seen clearly and their causes recognized, they need not result in confusion.

Performance appraisals should be used more for spotting strengths and weaknesses, and devising appropriate development programs, than as reward and punishment exercises. Long- and short-term goals should be identified, and because strategic alliances operate in environments that change quickly, these objectives and related criteria should be reassessed regularly.

Special training for alliance staff can make all the difference. Large companies tend to have in-house programs, while smaller companies tend to go outside for staff training. Whichever route your company takes, make sure all training is relevant to the actual tasks your people will be carrying out.

At all costs, do not allow your strategic alliance to become a dumping ground for incompetent personnel. Make it clear to those involved that their work is vital to the company's interests, and that effective performance will be rewarded.

The Right Stuff

"Effective international managers may be a rare breed, but they do exist." According to Paul Evans, a professor at INSEAD, good international managers are comfortable with managing and channeling diversity.

"Good international managers are created by diversified experience," Evans says. "When people work across frontiers they begin to recognize that certain things are no longer accepted wisdom." And differences exist not only in terms of markets and areas of particular strengths and weaknesses, but also in basic concepts concerning management and organization.

The good international manager is one who can reach beyond his own conditioning to share in a different way of seeing. What is needed is more than the exalted generalists produced by jumping from one multinational operation to another. "All that type of experience does is reinforce the individual manager's stereotypes of the people he or she is meeting, or meant to be managing."

While diverse experience is important, so is taking the time to build
relationships and understand the unique cultures within the alliance.

Motivating

How will you alter your incentive system to conform to the new dimensions of
your strategic alliance? It is no secret that conflicting or anti-productive incentives
can seriously undermine cooperative initiatives. It is important that you create an
environment where alliance success reflects individual success. A well-structured
incentive program that includes both financial and nonfinancial rewards will go
a long way to ensure that personal goals correspond to corporate goals.

And yet it is surprising how many firms leave conflicting incentives in
place. For example, if a technologist is rewarded for developing new patents, and
he is assigned a new role in an alliance that involves sharing information with his
counterparts, changes will have to be made in the way he is rewarded for his
work. Otherwise, if he carries out his new task, he could be hurting his own
chances of developing a new patent.

Perhaps he could be awarded the same amount for successfully completing
his alliance-related assignment as he is rewarded for developing a new patent.
Companies usually have quite a bit of leeway to structure benefit packages so
that both corporate and personal goals are recognized.

Large and small firms may require different types of incentives. In the large
firm, the group or division in charge of the alliance should have a stake in the
small company's success. This group can encourage the rest of the company to
buy into the alliance by passing along advantages and new expertise gained from
the alliance to other units. The champion must develop an incentive scheme that
encourages risk-taking and rewards success.

A small firm allied with a large partner usually has a natural motivation,
since cooperation probably means access to a much larger market—either by
selling directly to its partner or through its partner's distribution system. However, since small firms are unlikely to have a single alliance champion, senior
management's compensation should be tied directly to alliance success.

Coordination and Communication

A simple organizational structure is often most effective. In fact, business in
general is seeing a trend toward organizations with fewer levels of hierarchy and
less bureaucracy. This trend is particularly suited to strategic alliances because it
encourages communication between employees and firms.

Some companies have successfully adopted a team approach in which
people with critical functional expertise form a team and work closely with the

other company's team on alliance-related tasks. Each company contributes specialists from its particular areas of strength.

This approach not only devotes human resources to work exclusively on the alliance, it also creates the perfect opportunity for people to buy into the alliance at an early stage in the alliance-building process.

Using the team approach, members meet regularly as a group and individually as required. This way all the members of the project understand the obstacles and triumphs that the team is encountering. It provides a forum for frequent communication, ensuring that all members understand the issues, and helps to forge a team spirit.

Companies may choose to place more emphasis on the role of the champion. Staff are encouraged to develop direct links as the relationship progresses. The champion is informed as to the outcome of discussions. Many companies develop a sophisticated communication infrastructure, which identifies key people in different areas.

Careful attention should be paid to fostering mutual trust and joint commitment in an alliance. Exchange programs have been rated highly by participants and sponsors for short-term efforts that involve both companies or for longer-term, cross-cultural training programs.

In a joint venture, it is often an excellent idea if the general manager of the venture consults with senior management in both parent companies on major decisions, whether or not they have any real expertise in the particular issue at hand.

Those consulted are reassured by their continuing involvement, and are far more likely to be onside when the actual decision is made. The inclusion of key phrases or special concerns voiced by them can sometimes make all the difference.

Many experienced executives have stressed that there can never be too much communication. Otherwise, a good deal of time and money is wasted as

Communication Plan:

- Staff visits
- Informal meetings
- Exchanges
- Teleconferences
- Designate company contact point
- Dissemination of information

managers backtrack to the point of some misunderstanding, and try to establish a workable solution. This kind of disruption can result in employees sitting idle and losing their enthusiasm for the project. Lack of communication also obstructs the interaction upon which alliance synergies are based.

Is Your Company Ready to Communicate?

Is your corporate culture favorably disposed toward alliances? It goes without saying that your alliance team must be fully committed to the project, but what about the attitudes of the rest of the company? Your company will need to promote a long-term, positive attitude among all those who work with and within the alliance structure. For example, the activities of the alliance should be viewed as just as important as those of a subsidiary.

Have you created an organizational structure that will support the proper functioning of the alliance? Have you designated contact points at all levels within your company and the alliance?

How is information disseminated and absorbed within each firm? How will the information be shaped and who will receive it? It is important to keep in mind that how information is interpreted and distributed will have a powerful effect on alliance activities and on the attitudes people bring to bear on them.

Have you set up appropriate ways for participants to meet? Have you considered formal or informal meetings, staff visits or exchanges, or teleconferencing?

There are different schools of thought concerning how much and what kinds of communication are appropriate between a joint venture and its parents. Some managers believe that joint ventures fail when parents do not provide enough nurturing during their formative years. They feel joint venture activities should be carefully supervised and supported by the managers.

Other managers feel joint ventures tend to be smothered to death by overprotective, interfering parents who are unable to trust the new child. Or it may be that the parameters of communication and the purpose of the relationship need to be better defined. For example, managers in a large parent company may deluge a small joint venture with more requests than it can handle.

Sometimes the attempted solution to this problem is worse than the disease: managers in the parent company, frustrated that they are not getting the response they expected, add new layers of managers to the venture, and what was once intended as a small, flexible vehicle becomes yet another bureaucracy.

Endowing a strategic alliance with sufficient resources—a strong president, a full business system of its own (R&D, manufacturing, marketing, sales, and distribution), complete decision-making power on operating issues, a powerful board, and a sense of identity—is the best way of ensuring its survival. Decisions about equity financing and management structure can reside with parent companies, but operating decisions should be made by alliance managers whose sole responsibility is the joint venture.[1]

Exceptions to this rule include some R&D alliances, where parents have to retain a degree of control over the direction of joint-venture operations in order to ensure that the programs are in tune with their customer's needs.

In order to adapt to the new demands of strategic alliances, some companies have restructured themselves. In one case, the vice president for indirect marketing looks for the right partners, promotes the company both internally and externally, does the initial negotiations, manages contractual relationships, and provides guidance on sales and marketing approaches.

The business manager of this company spends time with the partner, assists on initial sales and marketing efforts, coordinates resources, is locally based, and understands business practices.

The technical support position provides technology transfer, does technical training, puts people on-site during the start-up period, provides telephone support on an ongoing basis, and consults on the internationalization of technology. An alliance cannot face more optimal conditions than having commitment from both operational and policy levels.

Designate Clear Contact Points

Aware of the complexity of their interaction, International Computers Ltd. of the UK and Fujitsu Ltd. of Japan have designated four levels of management interface, boosted by frequent exchanges of technical staff.

Xerox and Fuji Xerox have paired off personnel from every area and function of their companies. They have established an advisory executive resident at each other's headquarters, and they have formed joint task forces that get together regularly.

Many European and American multinational corporations have formed central liaison units to coordinate their strategic alliance relationships. This function may be independent, or it may be assigned to an existing division such as the strategic planning group or international affairs. Ford Motor Co. has gone as far as to set up a liaison office in Hiroshima to coordinate its activities with its equity partner, Mazda Motor Corp.

---

1   Joel Bleeke and David Ernst, "The Way to Win in Cross-Border Alliances," *Harvard Business Review*, November-December 1991, p. 132.

Conflict Resolution

"You can never afford to surprise your partner. You must treat him like a customer. That means you have to talk a lot. Things you might normally do as reflex or routine you have to explain and be prepared to change."
     Richard Dulude, Group President of Corning.
     Source: "The Business Column," C. Leadbeater, Financial Times, January 22, 1990.

A good deal of thought should be put into anticipating and resolving conflicts. No matter what formal methods you implement, both sides should remember that disagreements are inevitable and that circumstances will change. The ability to adapt to changes and to find intelligent compromises is invaluable. Flexibility is more important than any formal method of conflict resolution. Some disputes can also be avoided through the clear delineation of responsibilities.

Since legal systems differ so greatly, using the justice system to settle disputes with international partners is problematic. It is better to look at other means of averting or resolving conflicts. Solid lines of communication go a long way to solving this problem. Communication during the negotiation stage anticipates potential problems, with the result that formal methods of resolving them are established. Communication allows managers to become involved the moment conflicts arise. Often they can resolve problems then and there, before they have a chance to fester.

When alliance managers are unable to resolve disputes, a number of different recourses can come into play. Some managers refer the conflict to the people who were in charge of the negotiation process, who then examine the original agreement.

Some firms rely on the friendship between senior executives to work out conflicts. The weakness of this approach is that it may fall apart if one of the key figures leaves. Other companies set up a conflict resolution committee drawn from both firms to hear the issues and pass judgment.

The use of a predetermined third party to serve as a tie-breaker has been widely recommended. Such a person should be known and respected by all parties involved. Some executives dislike the idea of referring major strategic decisions to disinterested parties, complaining that these parties have nothing at stake in the alliance. Others believe having the option to slough off responsibility to a third party leads companies to give up too quickly on resolving conflicts in-house. The result, they say, is wasted resources, and placing vital interests in the hands of less involved, less knowledgeable persons.

Large and small companies often have different sorts of conflicts. Large firms will have both external and internal conflicts to manage. Various divisions or departments of the company may not look favorably on the alliance. And large firms may have problems coordinating daily operational activities with small firms that are more entrepreneurially focused.

Small firms may be surprised to find that their larger partners' needs are inconsistent with their own strategic goals. Or they may find their operating procedures are too simplistic to handle the complexities of the larger firm. Or the small firm may find itself overwhelmed with "help" sent in by the larger partner.

Interpretation problems can arise as well. For example, a firm may believe it has manufacturing rights to an entire product line, when such was not the intent of its partner.

Whatever the problem, if negotiators and upper management are on the lookout for potential conflicts, they will be able to resolve most before they become serious, or even alliance-threatening. Forethought and flexibility are the vital ingredients.

Conflict is not always bad. One multinational division president remarked that there should be occasional complaints from counterparts about employees who are unwilling to share information. These complaints can be an indication that gatekeepers are doing their job by controlling the release of peripheral or questionable information.

A certain amount of conflict can also mean ideas are fully considered before they are carried out. When a relationship is healthy, disagreements can be treated more lightly: they can be viewed as opportunities for cooperative efforts that will create improvements.

Performance Measurement

Monitoring the results of alliances enables firms to assess and improve their performance. It also allows companies to end alliances when predetermined objectives

---

How Ready Are You to Resolve Conflicts?

- Are you prepared to reach a compromise? Remember to get something in return!

- How solid are your communication links?

- Can conflict be resolved by direct reference to the original alliance agreement or a MOU?

- Are you prepared to attempt more-informal ways of resolving your conflict?

- Have you considered training staff in effective listening, interpersonal skills, negotiation, and conflict resolution techniques?

have been met, or to withdraw from unsuccessful alliances before serious harm occurs.

Most companies do not adequately monitor the performance of their alliances. Often they do not even have a clear idea of the levels of performance that were expected in the first place.

A successful alliance meets the expectations of its partners. It is important that each partner define its criteria for success. And while the alliance manager should have a clear sense of the strategic objectives of the alliance as an integrated whole, a clear understanding of the different priorities of each partner will add clarity to the assessment process, as well as help to avoid unpleasant surprises. These criteria may also change over time due to the growth of the importance of the strategic alliance or to changes in the market.

Criteria for judging alliances include objective factors such as profitability, growth in sales, market share, ability to meet margins, return on investment, and capital intensity. Objective criteria can be measured and quantified.

There are special problems involved in collecting and assessing alliance-related data. Data on the alliance needs to be differentiated from data pertaining to the parent companies. Eventually, the information-gathering systems involved may have to be separated.

This is especially true as the strategic importance of an alliance grows. Special attention should be paid to accounting and to financial reporting procedures. Separating costs and assets that are shared can be frustrating, but the process is a worthwhile one, for it enables you to ensure that the alliance remains on track.

Qualitative criteria can be just as vital to the assessment of an alliance. An important criterion for assessing the success of an alliance is often what was learned from the alliance. An alliance may be valued because it adds to company prestige or because it helped the company gain the confidence of the financial community.

Improvement in strategic position, improved relations with other firms, enhanced product recognition, improvements in the quality of a product, and the building of a long-term profit base are all important alliance accomplishments. Sometimes alliances may be unsuccessful in terms of objective criteria, but nevertheless still meet the essential goals of a partner.

Worldwide Markets

Strategic alliances have been hailed as the competitive tool of the 90s. Their rise to prominence parallels the emergence of powerful trading blocs and the globalization of the world's economies. This is no coincidence.

Globalization has resulted in a hyper-competitive environment in which only the strong, the swift, the innovative, and the adaptable survive. As national borders give way to free trade agreements and single-market models, companies are finding it harder to hide behind tariffs and artificial trade barriers.

Performance Measurement Criteria

- Are the criteria used for measurement related to the circumstances of the alliance rather than those of the parents?

- Were both long- and short-term objectives considered when drawing up the measurement criteria?

- How often will alliance performance reviews be made?

- Who will make the assessment? What training will they receive? Will the management teams from the parent firms be involved?

- Are performance reviews in tune with changes in the objectives or the operating conditions of the alliance?

Strategic alliances are perfectly suited for this do-or-die competitiveness. For small and medium-sized companies they are often the only way to compete with established, resource-rich multinationals. By allying themselves with foreign manufacturers, R&D labs, or marketing networks, North American SMEs can leverage their strengths and enter global markets on an equal footing with giant corporate and industry players.

For large companies like General Electric (GE) or International Business Machines (IBM), strategic alliances are ways to bypass cumbersome infrastructure and react more quickly to rapidly changing markets. Alliances are also good ways for large companies to establish supplier loyalties.

Strategic alliances are especially effective for penetrating the vast and powerful European Economic Community (EC) and Asia-Pacific markets.

The EC has formed a number of community-wide economic development programs that can only be accessed by EC firms—or their partners. The Asia-Pacific region has remained largely immune to the recession that gripped Europe and North America in 1990. The region has vast stores of capital which, in many cases, can only be accessed through strategic alliances.

In addition, the global economy will likely be dominated by European, Asia-Pacific, and North American trading blocs through the 1990s and into the twenty-first century. Companies active in all three markets will prosper. Companies shut out of these markets, for whatever reason, will fail. Knowing how to structure and manage strategic alliances gives North American companies a definite edge in an increasingly competitive world.

PART II

THE EUROPEAN ECONOMIC COMMUNITY

CHAPTER 7

THE OPPORTUNITY

- **THE EC MARKET AND ITS POTENTIAL**
- **POPULARITY OF ALLIANCES ON THE RISE**
- **EC POWER GROWING**
- **THE FUTURE IS NOW**

The EC Market and Its Potential

The emerging European Community (EC) Single Market presents North American businesses with an opportunity to profit from a dynamic new market. Those who enter it will enhance their ability to compete both at home and abroad.

Both North American and EC firms have found that strategic alliances are particularly well suited to the quickly changing, highly competitive, and varied conditions found in the EC. Because North Americans and Europeans share a common cultural heritage and similar managerial practices, transatlantic alliances are relatively easy to implement.

Diagram 9   Map of Europe

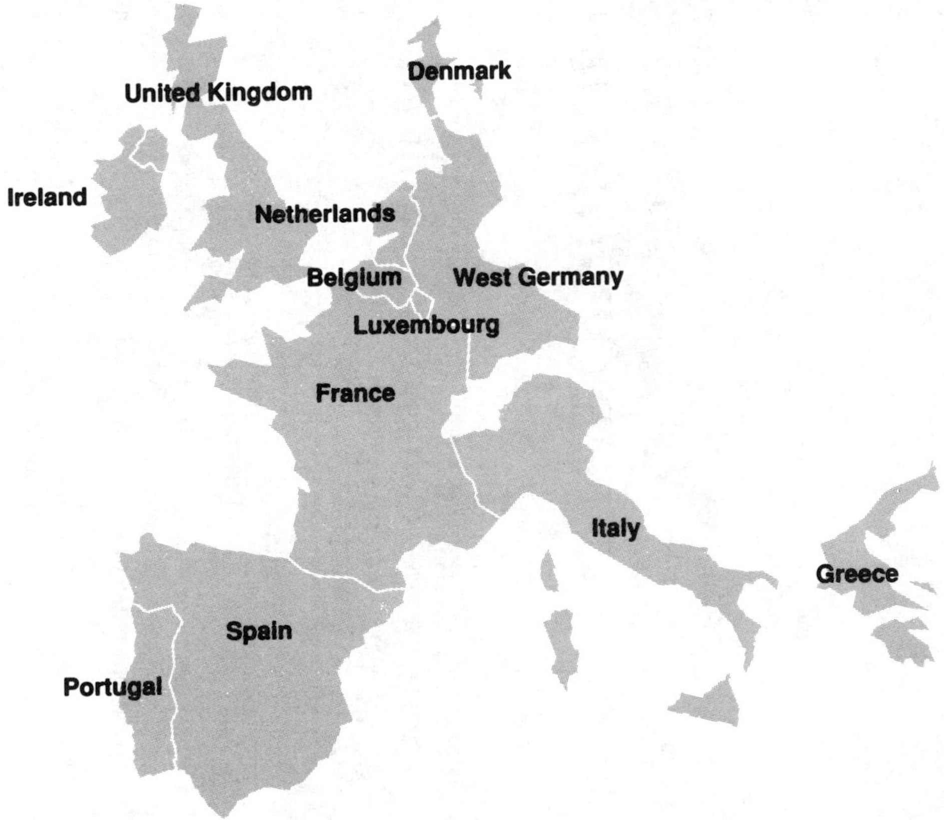

Entering the sophisticated markets of the EC is a challenging undertaking. Strategic alliances have become popular among companies because they provide many ways to turn the challenges of the EC market into competitive advantages. Non-EC firms are finding that strategic alliances are often the most effective way of penetrating that market.

Strategic alliances give firms access to additional resources and capabilities by sharing the high costs and risks of business, by participating in a division of labor appropriate to respective business strengths, and by better leveraging financial resources. Partners can contribute established marketing and distribution systems, as well as knowledge of the markets they serve. They ensure products get to market more quickly and more effectively.

EC partners can also give valuable advice on how to modify a product to meet local regulations and market preferences. They can help with such issues as obtaining product registrations and complying with packaging regulations. Using alliances inside the EC, even small North American firms can compete effectively in the large and diverse EC marketplace. Any linkages formed are restricted primarily by the company's ability to manage the relationship.

U.S. and Canadian companies will find European firms of all sizes open to partnering. Large European firms are favorably disposed to strategic alliances for

---

European Trading Power

The emerging EC Single Market rivals the United States in importance: it is the world's single largest trading bloc.

- The members of the EC are Belgium, Denmark, France, Germany, Greece, Ireland, Italy, Luxembourg, the Netherlands, Portugal, Spain, and the United Kingdom.

- The EC accounted for approximately 19.7 percent of world imports in 1990 (excluding intra-EC trade), compared to 14.3 percent for the U.S., 6.5 percent for Japan, and 3.3 percent for Canada.

- The EC's share of world exports in 1990 was approximately 19.6 percent (excluding intra-EC trade), compared to 11.4 percent for the U.S., 8.2 percent for Japan, and 3.8 percent for Canada.

- The Gross Domestic Product (GDP) of the EC in 1990 was $6.8 trillion, ahead of the U.S. figure of $6.4 trillion, and far ahead of Japan's $3.4 trillion.

historical reasons. European competition laws are traditionally much less restrictive than those in North America, allowing large corporations more latitude for cooperation.

Strategic alliances are also common among the many family-owned, small and medium-sized firms in Europe.

Research and development partnerships have played an important role in enhancing the competitiveness of EC corporations. Innovation in products, processes, marketing, and management has become the basis for competitive advantage. With the costs and risks of R&D skyrocketing, EC companies have made extensive use of R&D alliances, pooling their skills and resources in order to achieve technological excellence.

Production and marketing agreements have meant EC firms have been able to use the emerging Single Market for competitive advantage. Production agreements have allowed many European firms to achieve economies of scale and to offer a wider range of products than they could on their own. Marketing agreements have enabled them to make use of each other's distribution systems and knowledge of local markets.

Airbus Industrie: A New World-Class Competitor

One of the most durable joint ventures in the commercial aircraft industry is the Airbus Industrie, which brings together seven major EC firms, including the engine and airframe "national champions" of France (SNECMA & Aérospatiale), Britain (Rolls Royce and British Aerospace), Spain (Casa) and Germany (MBB via Deutsche Airbus).

The Airbus Industrie was formed in the 1960s to develop a commercial aircraft for the European market, and it has gone through many changes, including the withdrawal of British participation in 1969, the entry of Dutch and Spanish participants, and the return of the British in 1979. It was during this period that the A300 was developed. In the 1980s, two new aircraft, the A310 and A320, were introduced and work was begun on the A330/A340, thus rationalizing the product line and establishing Airbus Industrie as a credible supplier of a family of medium-range aircraft in a variety of sizes. The consortium became a world class competitor in the 1980s, and currently accounts for over a quarter of worldwide orders.

There is a high level of participation in Airbus by U.S. and Canadian companies. For example, in order to meet the need for a more flexible production capacity and take precautions against the fluctuations of the dollar, the major European partners concluded huge subcontracting agreements in 1988 with Bombardier and the U.S. companies Textron and Allied-Signal.

Airbus is actively looking for new Canadian partners. The European industry is also involved in most of the major private sector programs in the U.S., through shareholding and subcontracting agreements.

Of course, there are inevitable problems that arise in managing an alliance between North American and European firms. Different languages, legislative frameworks, market structures, customer preferences, business cultures, and communication and transportation costs are the most common problems encountered by Canadian and U.S. alliance partners in Europe.

Executives report that distance and some level of initial mistrust from the European side are the most difficult problems they have faced in forming alliances. But these problems have not detracted from the benefits North American firms have garnered from cooperative activities in the EC.

Popularity of Alliances on the Rise

Europeans fully recognize the crucial role strategic cooperation between firms is playing in the development of their industries. During the 1980s, the number of strategic alliances formed by European firms increased dramatically.

For example, between 1980 and 1989, European firms in biotechnology, information technologies, and advanced industrial materials developed 1,833 new strategic alliances. And that figure does not include more than 1,000 R&D alliances developed under EUREKA and EC programs such as ESPRIT, RACE, and BRITE.

The EUREKA program is of particular interest, since it is both well-funded and open to non-European firms. EUREKA alone has arranged more than 250 R&D consortia, while ESPRIT has more than 500 consortia to its credit.

IAF BioChem

IAF BioChem, a small Canadian biotechnical company, has entered into a strategic alliance with a British-based multinational giant, Glaxo Holdings PLC. Glaxo has 38,000 employees and an annual R&D budget of over $1.2 billion. IAF BioChem may be small, but it has a strong R&D base: 60 of its 80 employees are involved in R&D and 40 of these have Ph.D.'s. The alliance will use Glaxo's financial, marketing, and technical power to bring IAF BioChem's leading-edge products to an international market.

IAF BioChem produces drugs, vaccines, fine chemicals, and diagnostic kits. The company was started in 1986 by a group of scientists who bought the pharmaceutical facilities of the Armand Frappier Institute at the University of Quebec in Laval, just north of Montreal. They hold 10 percent of the shares, while two institutional investors, the Quebec Savings and Investment Fund (Caisse de depot et de placement du Quebec) and the Solidarity Fund of the Quebec Federation of Labor, hold a majority of the shares.

IAF BioChem announced its strategic alliance with Glaxo early in 1990. Under the terms of the alliance, the British corporation paid $15 million for exclusive rights to BioChem's new anti-AIDS drug throughout the world except for the U.S. and Canada. The two companies are working together on the preclinical research for the drug. It has been selected by the U.S. National Cancer Institute in 1990 as the best and most promising candidate to replace AZT, a drug notorious for its side effects.

In November 1990, the agreement between the two companies was extended to include another promising BioChem drug, this time an anti-cancer drug. It too is less toxic and more effective than any other existing compound of its type. The two companies have formed an R&D and marketing joint venture. Glaxo paid $25 million for a 10 percent equity interest in the joint venture, and has a two-year option for another 10 percent of IAF BioChem's shares.

Strategic Alliances in Biotechnology, Information Technologies, and Advanced Industrial Materials with at Least One European Partner

Year	No. of Alliances
1980	10
1981	25
1982	55
1983	85
1984	110
1985	205
1986	230
1987	247
1988	404
1989	406

Source: LAREA/CEREM database.

Diagram 10 Top European Countries

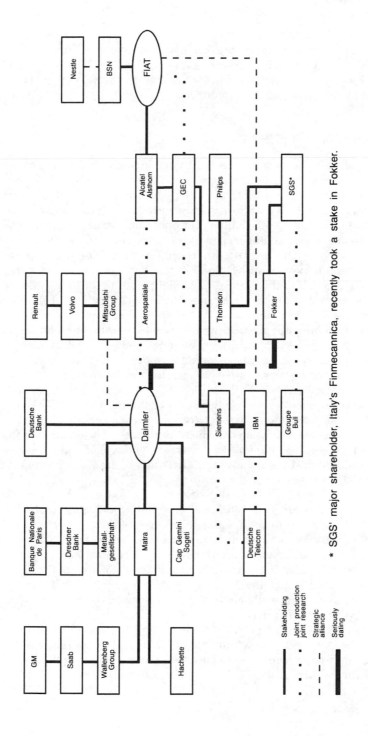

* SGS' major shareholder, Italy's Finmecannica, recently took a stake in Fokker.

Ref. *Forbes*, May 11, 1992

A recent report in *Forbes* magazine has gone as far as saying that Europe's top companies are no longer competing, but cooperating. The chart below shows that top European companies are swapping shareholdings, merging subsidiaries, and pooling research—and even production.

EC Power Growing

The EC is already the world's largest trading bloc, accounting for approximately 20 percent of world trade (excluding intra-EC trade).

After integration, the EC market of 342 million will offer substantial economies of scale to manufacturers. Lower production costs and a broader consumer base will increase the ability of European industry to compete more effectively both in Europe and in global markets. Large companies will be able to take advantage of economies of scale, while smaller companies will have improved access to community-wide niche markets.

One indication of the business potential posed by the Single Market initiative is the array of European countries that want to be linked in one way or another to the EC. The countries of the European Free Trade Association (EFTA) and the EC are presently negotiating the establishment of a common European Economic Area (EEA). In addition, over the next few years many Eastern European countries will become associate members of the Community.

The EFTA consists of Austria, Finland, Iceland, Norway, Sweden, and Switzerland. In December 1990, the EC and the EFTA reaffirmed their commitment to signing an agreement to establish the EEA by the summer of 1991. The EEA will lead to even deeper economic ties between the participants.

The conclusion of such an agreement would result in a market of more than 375 million people, with minimal trade barriers, and would add an estimated one trillion dollars to the EC's already large GDP (four of the six EFTA countries have a higher GDP per capita than Germany).

The EEA would not only allow for the free movement of capital, goods, services, and labor amongst the signatories, but would also result in the harmonization of competition policy and taxes; the simplification of border-crossing procedures; and special treatment of disadvantaged areas and groups of people.

While these negotiations are progressing, they have been complicated by differing views held by EFTA countries concerning the nature of the EEA: Austria and Sweden tend to see the EEA as an interim step to full EC membership (Austria has already formally applied), whereas Switzerland and Iceland tend to see the EEA as an end in itself.

In the latter half of the 1980s, the EC and the countries of Central and Eastern Europe concluded a number of trade and cooperation agreements, providing for trade benefits and financial assistance. Following the internal changes in Eastern Europe, the EC is now replacing these pacts with the more comprehensive "Europe Agreements." These will allow for deeper economic, political, and cultural ties.

The EC has also played a prominent role in the creation of the European Bank for Reconstruction and Development, which provides loans for projects in Central and Eastern Europe. Ultimately, the EC expects that closer cooperation will lead to formation of a continental free trade zone.

As a result, many firms are seriously considering using plants in Central and Eastern Europe as platforms for markets in both parts of the continent. General Electric (GE) bought the Hungarian manufacturer Tungsram, thus positioning itself to produce light bulbs for all of Europe. General Motors (GM) is investing $200 million in Hungary and Czechoslovakia to produce motors for Opel cars, while Asea Brown Boveri has purchased a turbine manufacturer in Poland.

Czechoslovakia, Hungary, and Poland all have a large number of scientists and technicians, and a highly skilled work force that is available at a fraction of Western costs. Thus, access to additional European markets beyond 1992 is an added incentive for North American businesses to take advantage of the move to a single market.

The Future Is Now

Companies have already been positioning themselves for 1992. As long ago as October 1989, Frans Andriessen, the EC's external relations commissioner, told journalists: "For most Europeans, especially our businessmen, 1992 is already here. It is happening now. The simple statistic that the increase in Community investment (in 1990) was 7 percent, the highest for two decades, illustrates the galvanizing effect that the program is having on our economy." The move to a Community-wide market has already stimulated fierce competition. Many companies are unable to compete under these new conditions and are disappearing. Those that do prosper are emerging as powerful competitors in markets throughout the world.

Participating in the EC can provide North American companies with a competitive edge in the U.S. and other markets. Those who stay home and ignore the European opportunity are running the risk of losing their market share to more aggressive companies that have developed the skills and technologies needed to compete anywhere in the world.

European Firms are Emerging as Powerful International Competitors

The emerging Single Market is creating a new breed of European global competitors intent on penetrating North American markets. For example,

Bull, the French computer company, has bought its computer businesses from Zenith and Honeywell. The Swiss food giant, Nestlé, and the Anglo-Dutch conglomerate, Unilever, have also been staking claims. Nestlé acquired RJR-Nabisco's candy divisions, nearly doubling its share of the U.S. candy market, while Unilever made $2 billion in new acquisitions in the U.S., carving out the third largest share of the U.S. cosmetics market.

Growth of Retail Sales Volume (1985=100)

	EC	U.S.	JPN	CAN
1980	94.9	83.3	90.4	91.8
1981	94.9	83.8	92.1	91.3
1982	94.9	83.1	92.9	86.3
1983	94.9	89.0	93.7	89.0
1984	97.2	95.4	96.6	93.0
1985	99.9	100.0	99.8	99.9
1986	104.7	105.7	106.4	104.6
1987	109.0	108.3	113.6	110.1
1988	112.4	112.2	122.7	113.8
1989	116.7	114.2	132.7	128.1

Note: EC figures (1980-89) include the 12 countries that were Member States in 1990.

Source: OECD Statistics, Paris (1991).

Growth in Real Gross Domestic/National Product (year-over-year percentage change)

	EC	U.S.	JPN	CAN
1980	1.5	−0.2	4.3	1.1
1981	0.2	1.9	3.7	3.4
1982	0.7	−2.5	3.1	−3.2
1983	1.6	3.6	3.2	3.2
1984	2.5	6.8	5.1	6.3
1985	2.4	3.4	4.9	4.7
1986	2.7	2.7	2.5	3.3
1987	2.7	3.4	4.6	4.0
1988	3.9	4.5	5.7	4.4
1989	3.5	2.5	4.9	3.3
1990	2.9	1.0	6.1	1.1

Note: EC figures (1980-89) include the 12 countries that were Member States in 1990.

Source: OECD Statistics, Paris (1991).

Diagram 11 Inflation Rates (year-over-year percentage change in consumer prices)

	1981	1982	1983	1984	1985	1986	1987	1988	1989	1990
Belgium	7.6	8.7	7.7	6.4	4.9	1.3	1.5	1.2	3.1	3.5
Denmark	11.7	10.1	8.9	6.3	4.7	3.7	4.0	4.6	4.7	2.6
France	13.4	11.8	9.6	7.4	5.8	2.5	3.3	2.7	3.5	3.4
Germany	6.3	5.3	3.3	2.4	2.2	-0.1	0.2	1.3	2.9	2.7
Greece	24.5	21.0	20.2	18.5	19.3	23.0	16.4	13.5	13.7	20.4
Ireland	20.4	17.1	10.5	8.9	5.4	3.8	3.1	2.2	4.0	3.4
Italy	17.9	16.5	14.7	10.2	9.2	5.9	4.7	5.1	6.2	6.5
Luxembourg	8.1	9.4	8.7	5.6	4.1	0.3	-0.1	1.5	3.4	3.7
Netherlands	6.8	8.9	2.8	3.3	2.2	0.1	-0.7	0.8	1.1	2.5
Portugal	20.0	22.7	25.1	28.9	19.3	11.7	9.4	9.6	12.6	13.4
Spain	14.5	14.4	12.2	11.3	8.8	8.8	5.3	4.8	6.8	6.7
U.K.	11.9	8.6	4.6	5.0	6.1	3.4	4.2	4.9	7.8	9.5
Canada	12.5	10.8	5.8	4.3	4.0	4.2	4.4	4.0	5.0	4.8
U.S.	10.3	5.2	3.2	4.3	3.6	1.9	3.7	4.0	4.8	5.4
Japan	5.0	2.7	1.9	2.3	2.1	0.6	0.1	0.8	2.3	3.1

Source: International Financial Statistics

CHAPTER 8

CREATING THE SINGLE MARKET

- **EC INTEGRATION**
- **THE LIBERALIZATION OF FINANCIAL SERVICES**
- **TOWARD MONETARY UNION**
- **COMPETITION AND ANTITRUST**
- **ALLIANCES VERSUS M&As**
- **ALLIANCE PATTERNS**

EC Integration

European integration is a complex process that affects all areas of economic and political life, including defense, education, human rights, and the environment. The key changes to be made are the elimination of physical, technical, and fiscal barriers, the liberalization of capital movements, and the establishment of a monetary union. The EC is also removing the protectionist measures that affect public procurement. It has already eliminated tariffs on trade between member countries.

Removing physical barriers primarily involves removing customs barriers and immigration and passport controls. Removing technical barriers involves the harmonization of technical regulations and standards through the adoption of Community-wide standards and the mutual recognition of a wide variety of national manufacturing and testing standards. All products will have to pass essential safety requirements, whether or not they are traded between EC countries. They can then be circulated freely throughout the EC. The industries most affected by technical trade barriers are:

- automobiles

- electrical and electronic equipment, including telecommunications

- machine tools

- pharmaceuticals and processed chemical products

- nonferrous mineral products

- metal products

- precision instruments and medical equipment

- transport equipment

- food and beverages

- leather goods

Removing fiscal barriers involves reducing the wide differences between value-added taxes (VAT) and between various excise duties. Most countries allow exports to be VAT-free, but imports are charged both VAT and excise taxes on a selective basis.

Patents and Trademarks

When the Community-wide patent system is adopted, applicants will no longer be subject to differing regulations and fees. Companies will no longer have to pay renewal fees in each country, while national working requirements will be replaced with the proviso that the Community patent be used in at least one member state.

These measures have been designed to complement the national systems rather than replace them, which means that patentees will have a choice between taking a national patent or a Community patent. When a company only needs to protect itself in two or three markets, it may be cheaper to get national patents in those specific countries rather than a Community patent.

Foreign companies would do well to register their trademarks in each country in which they trade. The EC has not yet adopted a new proposal that would provide for the creation of trademarks valid throughout the EC. The first Council directive aimed at harmonizing EC trademark laws was adopted at the end of 1988. It focused on approximating the terms of the member states' trademark laws that most directly affect the functioning of the internal EC market. These include giving the owners of trademarks "exclusive rights," permitting them to prevent others from using an identical or similar sign when this use creates the "likelihood of confusion" for consumers. When disputes arise, the laws of the member states apply.

The Liberalization of Financial Services

While there will still be some limits on international activities in the banking, securities, and insurance industries within the EC, extensive changes are being made.

The centerpiece of the 1992 program in the banking field is the Second Banking Directive, which will take effect on January 1, 1993. Under this directive, non-EC banks that establish a subsidiary in an EC member state will be able to receive a Community-wide banking license. The member state in which the bank's subsidiary is established will exert home-country control over the bank's affairs throughout the EC. The bank, in turn, will be free to open branches in other EC countries and to provide services within the range permitted by its EC home country.

The EC will apply the principle of "reciprocity" to banks from non-EC countries. That means that the EC will treat banks from a non-EC country the same way that it treats its own banks as long as that country does not discriminate against EC banks.

Initially, non-EC institutions were concerned that "reciprocity" would mean the EC would insist that its financial institutions abroad be permitted to carry out all the activities they are normally permitted to carry out within the EC—a range greater than is permitted in many countries. Critics warned that "reciprocity" measures of this kind would contribute to building a Fortress Europe. In the end, the EC did not go this route: reciprocity conditions seek only to ensure that EC institutions operating abroad receive the same treatment as local institutions.

Moreover, foreign banks established in the EC prior to 1993 will enjoy the same rights and treatment given EC banks. Thus, North American banks that have already established a subsidiary in the EC—that is, a firm with its own corporate identity and function, not just a representative office—are well positioned for the future.

As in banking, the EC Commission intends to establish a single insurance license that will enable companies legally established in one member state to offer their full range of products in another member state. There is, however, still some way to go.

Freedom to offer services covering large industrial and commercial risks has been increased through the Second Non-Life Insurance Directive, while the Second Life Insurance Directive enables individuals to go abroad to shop for the best prices and coverage. However, the freedom to go abroad for the best deals in non-life, life insurance, and private pension funds will apply to people who buy insurance, not to those who sell it.

Toward Monetary Union

The EC is now moving toward European Monetary Union (EMU). The European Monetary System (EMS), established in March 1979, represented a major step toward this goal. Since its inception, the EMS has largely fulfilled its goal of promoting price and exchange rate stability. It has also led to a convergence of the economic and monetary policies of the EC countries that participate in the Monetary System's Exchange Rate Mechanism. As a result, by 1989, most of the member countries were experiencing inflation rates below 6 percent.

The European Monetary System has three major components: the Exchange Rate Mechanism (ERM), which establishes predominantly fixed-exchange rates between the currencies of the participants; the European Currency Unit (ECU), which is a currency basket used at the center of the ERM; and credit facilities that supply credit when necessary to fulfill ERM obligations.

Each participating currency in the ERM is given a rate expressed in terms of the Ecu. A currency is then allowed to fluctuate on the market within a range of plus or minus 2.25 percent of its ECU rate or, in the case of the British pound sterling and the Spanish peseta, a range of plus or minus 6 percent of its ECU rate.

The European Monetary Union involves a more fundamental transfer of national sovereignty to the Community level than does the EMS. The first stage involves the elimination of barriers to the flow of capital, the membership of all EC countries in the ERM, and increased economic cooperation and coordination between them.

The second stage involves definition of a single monetary policy and the creation of a European Central Bank (EUROFED), which is tentatively scheduled for January 1, 1994. The final stage calls for the implementation of a single monetary policy and the creation of a common European currency.

Moving toward European monetary union is expected to reduce the uncertainty associated with multiple currencies, and consequently increase price stability. It will also reduce the costs of currency conversion within the EC—estimated at between $18.3 billion and $26.8 billion a year. In addition to having a positive economic impact on the Community, the process is a powerful symbol of the EC's successful drive toward economic integration, and of its desire for further political integration.

Competition and Antitrust

Originally, the European Commission could not block mergers and acquisitions prior to their taking effect, but it did have some powers to act after the event. During the 1980s, however, pressure mounted for increased authority to police mergers at the Community level before they occurred.

To this end, the Merger Control Regulation was adopted, going into force in September 1990. It was originally thought that joint ventures were excluded from the scope of this regulation, but this changed with the European Commission's ruling on the joint venture between Mitsubishi of Japan and Union Carbide of the U.S.

The Mitsubishi-Union Carbide Ruling: Joint Ventures Now Fall Under EC Merger Controls

On January 7, 1991, the European Commission ruled that a joint venture between Mitsubishi of Japan and Union Carbide of the United States did not contravene the anti-competitive regulations of the EC. By doing so, it brought joint ventures under the European Merger Control Regulations for the first time. It is also the first time the Commission has made a competition ruling on a deal between two non-EC firms.

The joint venture involved Mitsubishi purchasing a 50 percent share in Union Carbide's UCAR Carbon Company and its ten international subsidiaries. The joint venture is active in graphite, carbon, and related products.

The European Commission ruled that control of the joint venture rests with neither parent company and that neither parent company remains active as a producer or trader in UCAR's markets. The venture was therefore found to be compatible with EC competition policy.

The Merger Control Regulation monitors the potential anti-competitive effects of corporate concentration within the European Community, especially as 1993 approaches. The regulation's provisions apply only to those linkups, mergers, or acquisitions with a "Community dimension": where the aggregate worldwide turnover of all the undertakings concerned is more than $7.4 billion, and the aggregate Community-wide turnover of each of at least two of the undertakings concerned is worth more than $371.5 million.

The Commission must be notified within one week of the signing of an agreement or the launching of a tender offer. The Commission then has one month to decide if an investigation is necessary. And finally, the Commission has four months to investigate and provide a ruling on an agreement or tender.

The EC Committee of the American Chamber of Commerce in Belgium had this to say about the change: "Rather than see the Commission intervene *a posteriori* . . . and take the risk of being forced to back down from an already

Effects of the Key 1992 Changes

Removing physical barriers

- will free the movement of goods and services within Europe

- will assure that a product can enter any EC country, once it has entered one of them

Removing technical barriers

- will allow unhindered distribution to all EC countries once a product has met the technical standards of one EC country

- will allow industry to produce for a wider market

- will open the public procurement market to competition

Removing fiscal barriers

- will eliminate the wide differences in indirect taxes that distort trade between member states

Liberalization of capital movements

- will enhance competition and choice in financial services

- will make channeling savings into investment more efficient and less costly

- will give borrowers access to more diverse and cheaper financing for investment and trade within the EC

Monetary union

- will reduce the uncertainty of exchange rate fluctuations

- will save on the costs of currency exchange

- will facilitate intra-EC trade

- will increase price stability

effective concentration, business favors a rapid and confidential procedure by which Community-wide mergers could be definitely cleared by the Commission."[1]

Strategic Alliances versus Mergers and Acquisitions

Mergers and acquisitions (M&As) are a common way for companies to position themselves in the Single Market. M&As are particularly important for companies seeking greater economies of scale. In Europe, they allow EC companies to gain the size and diversity that will enable them to compete both at home and abroad with larger Japanese and North American firms.

Yet mergers and acquisitions in the EC need to be understood within a proper context. Firms in continental Europe tend to be smaller than their North American counterparts, and are more likely to be closely run family affairs. They also have a long history of cooperating to take on larger projects.

This makes them more predisposed to cooperative ventures than North American companies, and more hostile to foreign takeovers. Successful M&As in the EC tend to take place between firms that have known each other long enough for trust and respect to develop. For example, in the 1980s, the rate of domestic M&As among the largest 1,000 EC firms was about twice the rate of their cross-border M&A activity.

By the same token, strategic alliances between European firms from the same country tend to include equity arrangements more often than partnerships between firms from different member states. An even smaller proportion of strategic alliances between EC and non-EC firms involve equity.

British companies are not as suspicious of takeovers as are their continental cousins. Because their corporate culture, share structures, and accounting practices are similar to those of North America, M&As are easier in Britain than on the continent. For similar reasons, British firms interested in expansion have tended to look to North America.

If you want to acquire an EC firm, especially a continental one, it makes sense to develop a cooperative business relationship with it first. This gives both companies a chance to develop trust and respect for each other and to assess the real advantages and disadvantages of a merger or acquisition.

There are a number of other factors that make acquisitions in the EC more difficult than in North America. Because of unique share structures, stock swaps are impractical, and so acquisitions usually require cash. Accounting practices also vary—the necessary information is often hard to get, and valuations often require extensive investigation. Public companies in the UK, France, Germany, and Italy are well documented, but member states do not have information sources

---

1   Europe 1992 Working Group Report on Competition Policy, *EAITC*, January 1991.

Domestic and Cross-Border Takeovers: Different Motivations (in percentages)

Reasons For M&A	Domestic	Cross-Border
Entry to new markets	10	35
Horizontal expansion	20	25
Economies of scale	20	10
"Good buy"	20	10
Product diversification	13	10
Vertical expansion	7	5
Other	10	4

such as Standard & Poor's directories and Dun & Bradstreet reports or the American 10-K forms.

On the other hand, European banks take a more aggressive position in supplying information, assisting M&A activity, and directing margins than do banks in North America.

M&As require matching companies, corporate cultures, products, and distribution systems. Because so much depends on finding the right fit, they are slow to set up. Locating the acquisition can take two to five years—too long if the purpose is to take advantage of the quickly evolving Single Market.

The Farther From Home, the Fewer the Equity Arrangements (in percentages)

Type of Alliance	Intra-EC	EC–U.S.A.	EC–JAP	Total
No equity alliance	35.6	52.8	64.9	45.3
Joint venture	16.5	16.2	25.0	17.1
Minority holding	11.0	7.7	5.5	9.2
Majority holding	36.9	23.2	5.5	28.4
Number of cases	699	581	128	1408

Source: LAREA/CEREM database, 1980-89.

Diagram 12 Less Distance, More M&As: EC Mergers and Acquisitions, 1987/88

Sector	National		Community		International		Total	
	M	A	M	A	M	A	M	A
Industry	214	115	112	37	57	29	383	181
Distribution	40	13	8	4	9	5	57	22
Banking	53	38	12	15	13	28	78	81
Insurance	14	8	14	4	12	7	40	19
Total	321	174	146	91	91	69	558	303

Source: Commission of the European Communities, 1989.

And companies that want to cover more than one EC market may have to make more than one acquisition. For many companies this is uneconomical, especially when it is possible to develop as many as three strategic alliances for the cost of a single acquisition. In addition, a failed joint venture usually costs between 25 percent and 35 percent of the price of a failed acquisition.

M&As do make sense if a substantial amount of corporate revenue already comes from European markets. Otherwise, they tend to be too costly and time-consuming.

Strategic alliances, on the other hand, tend to be flexible instruments with a more far-reaching appeal to U.S. and Canadian companies seeking to take advantage of the EC Single Market.

Even when acquiring an EC firm does make good business sense, strategic alliances are often an important first step in the process.

Preserving Autonomy, Enhancing Competitiveness

Bioserae is a small French biotechnology firm involved in the research, development, and marketing of innovative pharmaceutical products. Faced with high R&D costs and a world market that is dominated by large multinational enterprises, Bioserae felt that it needed to find a large partner or allow itself to be absorbed by one of the giants, which could then supply the technical and financial resources needed to develop Bioserae's products.

Bioserae chose to protect its autonomy. It approached its main raw-materials supplier, the large French petrochemical company Elf Aquitaine. The resulting deal has benefited Bioserae both financially and technologically. Elf Aquitaine bought a minority holding (34 percent) in Bioserae and is also helping in the developmental stage of Bioserae's products.

Patterns in EC Alliance Formation

Alliance formation in the EC has changed dramatically in the last ten years. Alliances have become more complex and their functions have become more varied. By the end of the 1980s, there was an enormous growth in all types of alliances, but especially in the number of "multifunctional" alliances—alliances that include cooperation in R&D, production, and marketing. Most other alliances are agreements between firms concerning technical standards.

In the early 1980s, North American firms were the preferred partners of EC companies. By the mid-1980s this had begun to change, and since then EC firms have been increasingly forming alliances with other EC firms.

Americans Are the Favorite Non-EC Partners (percentage)

YEAR	U.S.	JPN	OTHER
1980	40.0	0	0
1981	30.4	13.0	8.7
1982	48.1	5.6	5.6
1983	51.5	5.5	7.7
1984	46.4	9.6	6.4
1985	47.0	9.3	7.8
1986	39.2	9.5	9.1
1987	28.1	5.6	10.8
1988	28.8	6.2	11.9
1989	30.1	6.8	14.3

Note: this data is based on a survey of 1833 firms.
Source: LAREA/CEREM (Paris).

Cross-Border Alliances in the European Steel Industry

In Europe, there has been a series of cross-border joint ventures in finishing capacity among small and medium-sized companies and the merging of interests in special and related steels. The purpose of the European agreements is most often to achieve economies of scale and to benefit from some rationalization. The anticipated downturn in steel demand across Europe in the early 1990s is expected to increase pressures on many companies to enter joint ventures or mergers.

European Alliances

Soliac (France)—Riva (Italy)
Soliac—Cockerill-Sambre (Belgium)
Soliac—Arbed (Luxembourg)
Cockerill-Sambre-Arbed

Over half the alliances between EC firms are multifunctional. While R&D alliances are common, EC firms tend to form few alliances that are focused only on production or marketing. Multifunctional collaboration is also common between EC and North American firms, and much of it includes equity arrangements.

In the past, alliances between Japanese and EC firms have focused more on production. Many of the initial Japanese plants in Europe were "screwdriver" plants that simply assembled components made elsewhere.

A recent trend sees Japanese companies setting up R&D centers in the EC. However, there is a fear they will be locked out of the EC Single Market unless they begin contributing more coveted, value-added industry.

Alliance patterns also differ from one industry to the next. For example, significantly more alliances in the biotechnology sector involve R&D than in the next largest R&D sector, information technologies. Marketing agreements, on the other hand, are far more important in the information technologies industry than in biotechnology or materials.

Alliances—More Complex and Diverse

Year	R&D	Production	Marketing	Global	Other
1980	0	2	0	3	0
1981	12	0	3	8	0
1982	19	9	8	18	0
1983	26	19	15	31	0
1984	28	25	19	49	4
1985	52	37	39	67	9
1986	73	32	27	90	10
1987	61	30	39	118	1
1988	81	41	84	186	10
1989	44	78	57	225	8

Figures indicate EC alliances formed outside EC alliance programs.

Note: Alliances that involve two functions (e.g., R&D and production, but not marketing) have been entered twice (under R&D and under Production), but alliances involving all three functions have been listed only once, under Global. The drop in the number of R&D and commercial agreements in 1989 reflects the movement toward global agreements rather than a movement away from any one of the categories.

Source: LAREA/CEREM database (Paris).

In addition, alliance patterns differ within each industry according to the location of the partners. In the information technologies industry, alliances between EC firms are more concerned with R&D. European-North American alliances, on the other hand, are often vehicles for penetrating either the North American trading block or the European Single Market.

EC-Japanese alliances in the information technologies sector are fairly evenly distributed between R&D, production, and marketing, although these alliances do not include all three functions nearly as often as do intra-EC and EC-North American alliances.

CHAPTER 9

EC STRATEGIC ALLIANCE PROGRAMS AND INITIATIVES

- **EC ALLIANCE PROGRAMS**
- **EC REGIONAL PROGRAMS**
- **USING REGIONS FOR COMPETITIVE POSITIONING**

European Alliance Programs

The EC itself has actively promoted the formation of inter-firm collaborative agreements since the early 1980s. As a result, EC firms have developed sophisticated collaborative skills, and are quick to recognize the strategic advantages of partnering. U.S. and Canadian firms looking for European partners will find that their job has been made that much easier.

The first European program to promote strategic alliances was the European Strategic Program for Research and Development in Information Technology (ESPRIT). It was launched in 1983, and is currently in its second phase. ESPRIT was followed quickly by RACE, a program that promotes strategic partnerships in the telecommunications industry.

Many others have arisen since. In order to participate, non-EC firms must have at least an EC subsidiary, and even then entrance is not guaranteed. North American firms have a better chance of accessing these programs through strategic alliances with EC firms, especially if the partnerships include some form of equity arrangement.

By contrast, EUREKA is open to non-European companies. Launched initially by the EC and EFTA countries in 1985, EUREKA is a well-funded program that has included a number of successful North American participants.

BRITE/EURAM, which stands for Basic Research in Industrial Technology for Europe and European Research in Advanced Materials, was founded in 1989 and will end in 1992. The program has a total budget of $648.4 million for the development of R&D consortia in advanced materials technologies, design methodology, and quality assurance for products and processes; application of advanced conventional manufacturing technologies and manufacturing processes for flexible materials (i.e., textiles); technologies for manufacturing processes; and aeronautics. Firms and universities established in either the EC or the EFTA countries are eligible.

RACE means Research and Development in Advanced Communications Technologies in Europe. The program is focused on integrated broadband communications (IBC) and the development of technology for commercial IBC services, to be introduced in 1995.

The RACE program is designed to lay the foundations of the Community's communications infrastructure. It covers all aspects of terrestrial networks, as well as satellites and mobile telecommunications. It involves all European telecommunications operators, service providers, and equipment manufacturers.

The 90 consortia established under the RACE program involve 306 organizations, including universities, telecommunications administrations, and private companies, 130 of which are small and medium-sized businesses. RACE 1 is scheduled to run from 1987 to 1992 and has a budget of $841.5 million. The RACE 2 budget is contained in the 1990-94 EC Framework Program, and will overlap with the end of RACE 1.

ESPRIT has been the largest, longest, and most successful of the EC programs to date.

ESPRIT 1, which lasted from 1984 to 1988, had a budget of $975 million. ESPRIT 2 began in 1988 and will last until 1992, with a budget of $2.3 billion.

The focus for ESPRIT is microelectronics, information processing systems, office and business systems, and computer-integrated manufacturing. The program is open to firms established in the EC and EFTA countries.

Successful ESPRIT Projects

The software production and maintenance support program is designed as a new type of information system for managing the development of software products. It was initiated by a number of medium-sized French firms, with Siemens of Germany as the prime contractor. When Siemens withdrew from the project in 1986, it was replaced by the French firm TECSI and a Spanish firm with which one of the partners had wanted to build closer ties. By the end, the project involved five small and medium enterprises (SMEs) and no large firms.

Automatic Control Systems

This project has contributed to the development of more-competitive microchip production equipment and systems. It also contributed to the implementation of new standards in its area. The technology involved is at the leading edge of automatic wafer fabrication sequence control systems for plasma etching. It was initiated by European Silicon Structures (ES^2), a consortium with its own wafer fabrication line. All of the partners, Societé Bertin (France), ES^2 (France), Leybold A.G. (Denmark), Mietec (Belgium), and Plasma Technology Ltd (UK), were SMEs.

The EUREKA Program was created in 1985 on the basis of a proposal by French President François Mitterrand. The current EUREKA program spans the years 1989 to 1992. EUREKA is not an EC program, and it has no central fund as is common among the EC programs.

Rather, the funds are contributed and administered by each of the 20 countries involved in the program. The countries pay a portion (usually less than one-third) of the costs of participation by their companies or research institutes. The members of EUREKA include the 12 EC countries, plus Sweden, Austria, Switzerland, Norway, Finland, Iceland, Turkey, and the EC Commission. EU-REKA is open to nonmember firms and institutes so long as they are in partnership with at least two European firms.

Several Canadian firms have joined EUREKA projects and several U.S. firms have joined the EUREKA Prometheus projects. The latter is the Program for a European Traffic with Highest Efficiency and Unprecedented Safety, which involves development of electronic road traffic and pollution control systems. IBM is involved in the JESSI project on semiconductors. French firms are involved in a biotechnology project with Argentinians.

Most EUREKA projects are focused on robotics, information technologies, environment, and biotechnologies, although there are a number of important projects in transportation, energy, and laser technology.

**Alliances Formed Through EC Programs
(As of Jan. 1, 1991)**

Program	Number of Alliances
ESPRIT	552
BRITE/EURAM	345
RACE	90
EUREKA	386

Source: LAREA/CEREM database, Paris.

EC Regional Programs

Companies choose a country, but they settle into a region or community. Today, firms know that their competitiveness is largely determined by the capabilities, infrastructure, and partnering opportunities of the regions in which they locate. The integration of European markets has led to the emergence of a number of regional powerhouses, the largest of which are known as the Four Motors of Europe: Baden-Württemberg in Germany, Catalonia in Spain, Lombardy in Italy, and the Rhône-Alpes in France.

All of these regions have been financial, industrial, trade, and cultural centers for centuries, and today they are all playing a vital role in securing the international competitiveness of the EC. All actively promote strategic alliances between local and foreign firms.

Baden-Württemberg

Perhaps the region with the most comprehensive approach, however, is Baden-Württemberg.

Baden-Württemberg's State Development Corporation (LEG) is an excellent example of the kind of support EC regions are beginning to give to outside firms. It assists foreign firms that intend to locate in Baden-Württemberg, or that intend to enter into cooperation with a company from the region. All LEG staff speak English, and its services are free of charge. They fall into five categories:

1. Partner Search

LEG has a list of more than 300 companies from the region that have indicated an interest in finding a partner, in some cases explicitly requesting that it be an

The 24 Most Competitive EC Regions

Rank	Sub-region (Region), Country
1	Darmstadt (Hesse), Germany
2	Oberaven (Hesse), Germany
3	Stuttgart (Baden-Württemberg), Germany
4	Hamburg, Germany
5	Ile de France, France
6	Karlsruhe (Baden-Württemberg), Germany
7	Luxembourg
8	Rheinland-Pfalz (Rhineland), Germany
9	Valle d'Aosta (Northwest), Italy
10	Berlin (West), Germany
11	Hovedstadsregionen, Denmark
12	Mittelfranken (Bavaria), Germany
13	Alsace, France
14	Düsseldorf (Westphalia), Germany
15	Greater London (Southeast), UK
16	Freiburg (Baden-Württemberg), Germany
17	Tübingen (Baden-Württemberg), Germany
18	Lombardy, Italy
19	Grampian (near Aberdeen, Scotland), UK
20	Liguria (Northwest), Italy
21	Schwaben (Bavaria), Germany
22	Rhône-Alpes, France
23	Köln (Westphalia), Germany
24	Emilia-Romagna, Italy

* The ranking was determined using four weighted variables: GNP/persons employed (25 %), GNP/population (25 %), unemployment (40 %), and employment potential (10 %).

Source: EC, 1987.

overseas firm. These companies come both from technologically oriented and consumer-goods industries.

If none of the firms on the list is suitable, then LEG conducts a targeted partner search among the region's industrial and trading companies, based on the specific needs of the foreign firm.

2. Location Search

LEG can propose a selection of specific sites to satisfy the needs of the foreign firm. The agency can then provide support in negotiating with the state and local authorities, including a discussion of financial incentives.

3. R&D Partner Search

LEG has experts in R&D management who can help firms define their needs and identify the research institute that has the right know-how and experience. They can provide contacts and support during subsequent discussions with research institute experts.

4. Supplier Search

LEG has industry experts who can provide a list of firms that manufacture the products an investor needs. It can put the investor in touch with the ones chosen.

5. General Product Support

LEG can also provide ongoing support during the entire course of a project. The agency's project managers can help firms not only in the planning stage but in their implementation too. They provide the necessary information and contacts, and support firms during negotiations with partners, public authorities and the banks, as well as helping put together financing packages.

The Four Motors are not the only industrial sectors in Europe. Other EC regions are worthy of consideration by any North American firm looking for European R&D or manufacturing bases.

These areas are likely to increase in importance throughout the 1990s. In the preamble to the EC treaty, the member states declared their aim of "reducing the differences existing between the various (industrial) regions and the backwardness of the less favored regions." The centerpiece for this action is the European Regional Development Fund, also known as the Regional Fund.

Access to the fund can be gained by participating in the national or regional programs within the EC member states. For example, through agencies such as France's DATAR, European governments offer attractive incentives (cash and tax relief) to businesses willing to invest in underdeveloped areas. By participating in

Industrial Sectors in Baden-Württemberg, 1988 (percentage of employees)

Mechanical engineering	18.2
Electrical engineering	17.5
Automobile manufacturing	15.9
Textile industry	4.8
Chemical industry	4.8
Production of iron, sheet and metallic goods	4.7
Food industry	3.8
Precision engineering, optics, and watchmaking	3.4
Production of plastic goods	3.4
Woodworking	2.7

Source: Ministry of Economic Affairs and Technology (State of Baden-Württemberg).

national or regional programs in the EC, North American firms can also take advantage of EC regional policy.

Using Regions for Competitive Positioning

With increasing international competitiveness and technological innovation, regional characteristics such as market proximity, the availability of a quality work force, technological excellence, stable operating costs, and an attractive quality of life have become vitally important.

As firms implement computer-integrated manufacturing (CIM) to cut costs and improve product quality, they are increasing their reliance on skilled engineers and technicians. For many firms, the quality of the work force can be more important than its cost. As a result, an important determinant of site location is proximity to educational institutions that can offer a steady supply of quality CIM engineers, technicians, and operators.

Moreover, whether active in advanced technology or in more traditional sectors, all enterprises are increasingly relying on processes that use advanced production technology. For this reason, the same locational factors are critical to both high- and low-technology producers.

High-technology manufacturing industries tend to locate in regions where networking to subcontractors is easy. The German company Mannesmann, one of

Diagram 13   Baden-Württemberg: At the Center of Europe

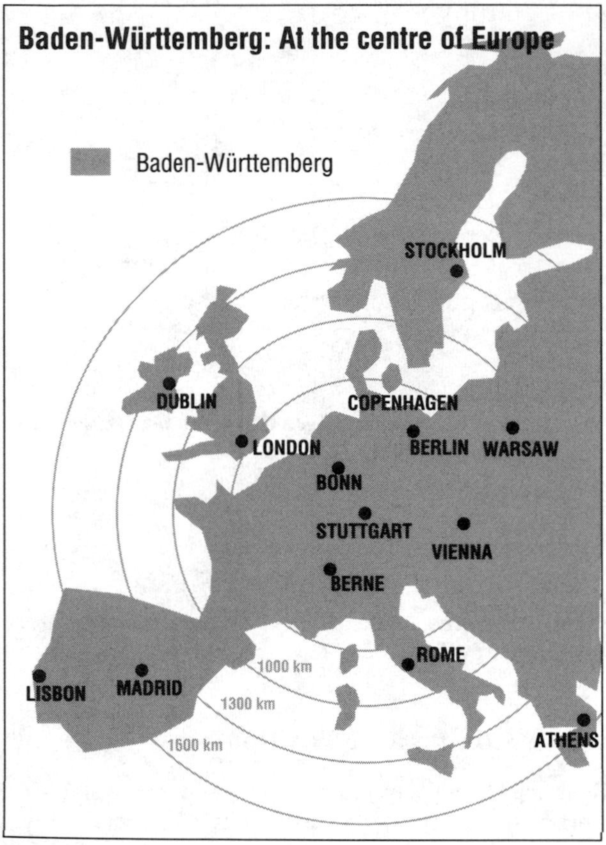

Baden-Württemberg: At the centre of Europe

the largest firms in the world in the mechanical (machine tool, hydraulic) industry, located its French subsidiary near Grenoble for this reason, developing supplier relationships with nearly 500 local firms. Hewlett-Packard has also located a manufacturing plant in Grenoble, developing ties to over 250 local subcontractors.

Firms interested in establishing production capabilities based on low cost labor are still going to Spain and Portugal, with Catalonia especially popular. Service-sector firms, including the headquarters of major multinationals, have been flocking to urban centers such as Milan, Paris, Brussels, London, Munich, and Paris; while financial capital is largely oriented toward Switzerland, Luxembourg, and the UK because of their developed financial infrastructures and flexible regulatory climates.

Key Factors for Assessing a Region:

1. good educational facilities and quality work force

2. efficient and skilled suppliers

3. communications and transportation infrastructure

4. technology supply

5. reliable energy supplies

6. an attractive quality of life that will keep skilled workers satisfied

---

For SMEs: European Economic Interest Groups

In 1989, the European Community created a new legal instrument that facilitates cross-border cooperation between small and medium-sized enterprises (SMEs) in such areas as R&D, purchasing, production, sales, and computerized data processing. The new instrument is known as the European Economic Interest Group. The EEIG is set up by contract rather than by incorporation. The Community regulation creating this instrument imposes only minimal obligations with regard to the organization and management of the group and allows for various financing arrangements. In fact, the regulation does not have a requirement that the grouping be formed with capital.

Through the use of EEIGs, small businesses can achieve economies of scale and reduce risks without the cost of setting up their own facilities, branches, or subsidiaries and without investing in the development, production, or marketing of the full range of products required for effective competition.

Non-EC firms may participate in EEIGs if they are already established and active in the Community. The official address of the EEIG must be in the EC, but the principal activity of the EEIG does not have to be located within the Community.

CHAPTER 10

ALLIANCE OPPORTUNITIES IN INDUSTRY SECTORS

- **AEROSPACE**
- **AUTOMOBILES**
- **BIOTECHNOLOGY**
- **ENVIRONMENT**
- **FINANCIAL SERVICES**
- **FOOD AND DRINK**
- **INFORMATION TECHNOLOGIES**

Certain EC industry sectors offer unique opportunities to North American companies seeking alliance partners. These are sectors in which North American companies have demonstrated strength, innovation, and competitiveness, and which are most likely to benefit from transatlantic alliances.

Aerospace

The European aerospace industry is the second largest in the world after the U.S., and far ahead of Japan. Traditionally, military aeronautics accounted for a majority of EC sales in the sector, but is now decreasing in importance.

On the other hand, the expanding product range of EC civil aeronautics has enabled EC industry to take advantage of a surge in sales, and growth in the European aerospace sector is expected to come mainly from civil aeronautics.

The European aerospace industry has had a large impact on the formation of the EC Single Market. Such programs as Airbus Industrie, Panavia, Arianespace, and the European Space Agency have played an important role in initiating the economic integration of Europe. The elimination of barriers to aerospace trade within the EC predates similar Single Market initiatives in other sectors.

Structure

European aerospace companies tend to be smaller and less profitable than their American counterparts. This difference in size has been a strong motivating factor behind cooperative action among them. Research and development alliances have enabled EC aerospace firms to address their high fixed-development costs.

Alliances have also helped to solve another problem. Perceptions of national self-interest had led to an overcapacity of aerospace production in Europe. The formation of international alliances in the EC led to the opening up of the competitive market. European Community industries are now competing in global markets, while their internal market is now a pan-European one.

Strategic alliances have made the EC industry much more competitive, and Canadian and U.S. companies are playing important roles in these alliances.

Canadian Aerospace Exports

The Canadian aerospace industry is highly export-oriented. Exports to the EC consist largely of sales of Pratt & Whitney (now owned by United Technologies) engines, Boeing Canada aircraft, and some proprietary products to original equipment manufacturers. Total exports will be boosted by Canadair's increasing sales of components to the European consortium Airbus. Another Canadian success story is Spar Aerospace, which developed the Canadarm and is a leader in space-station research and satellite communications.

Markets

There are five categories of products in the civil aerospace industry: commercial jets, commuter aircraft, helicopters, engines, and space equipment.

Fifteen years ago, the European industry accounted for only 4 percent of world orders in the commercial jet industry. In the late 1980s, it accounted for 25 percent of world orders, and deliveries should remain at the same level for years to come.

The Airbus line has had a major impact on this increase in production, but the production of aircraft with less than 100 seats, such as the British Aerospace BAe 146 and the Fokker 100, has also been expanding rapidly.

Europeans are also involved in the growth of American civil aircraft. For example, companies in the Italian, Spanish, and British industries have close associations with Boeing and McDonnell Douglas.

Small commuting planes equipped with turboprop engines for regional connections constitute a high-growth segment. This area is dominated by European industry, which supplied 65 percent of the world market in 1988. In terms of orders, from 1987 to 1988 the world market grew by 36 percent, to 18,323 seats, while deliveries increased by 23 percent in 1988 to 11,050.

The European helicopter industry is the world's largest exporter of helicopters, supplying more than one-third of the American market. In 1987, it delivered 392, of which 216 were for civil purposes. The peak year, 1982, saw 752 deliveries, while the low was 320 in 1985. Prospects for the EC helicopter industry are good, especially in exports. Aerospatiale, MBB, Westland, and Agusta are key companies.

The airplane engine product group has experienced consistent growth. Part of this growth is linked to the rise in European aircraft production, though a more immediate factor is orders for equipping American planes with engines that were co-produced in Europe. In this area, there are more transatlantic cooperation agreements than there are intra-European ones. Examples of transatlantic alliances are the CFM international consortium between Europe and the US for the CFM 56, and IAE between the US, Europe, and Japan for the V 2500 engine.

Space equipment includes both launch vehicles and satellites. While it plays a minor part in the overall industry, it is rising rapidly in importance. In 1980, European space equipment accounted for 3.1 percent of overall production; in 1987, it accounted for 6.1 percent. Consolidated turnover more than tripled from 1982 to 1987, rising from $644 million to more than $1.92 billion. Employment increased from 13,720 to 21,000 jobs.

This growth is linked to the production of application satellites. The Europeans had seven satellites in orbit from 1980 to 1984: 17 were put in orbit from 1985 to 1989. They have scheduled 20 for launch in the period 1990-1994. The largest growth factor in the space sector has been sales of launching services by the European firm Arianespace. Arianespace consists of the major European companies involved in the production of the Ariane rocket launcher. They launched 11 satellites from 1980 to 1984, 36 from 1985 to 1989, and they have 60 slated to go between 1990 and 1994.

Incentive Programs

The aerospace industry has been the beneficiary of massive government assistance, including direct financing of research and public orders. Airbus, for example, was heavily financed by national governments. On average, the total R&D of European companies in this sector amounts to 20 percent of sales, 7 percent of which is self-financed. For American companies, R&D represents 17 percent of sales, 4 percent of which is self-financed.

Outlook

Much of the EC aerospace production is still military. However, the military market for aerospace products has been declining due to reduced military budgets, improved East-West relations, and a technology cycle that is currently in transition, with second-generation weapon systems due sometime in the mid-1990s.

Fortunately, civil aeronautics looks exceptionally good for the medium-term, due to a sharp rise in air transportation and a growing need to renew the first generation of commercial jet airlines.

The EC industry is well aware of the technological abilities of North American aerospace companies, and is actively seeking U.S. and Canadian partners.

Automobiles and Automotive Parts

The emergence of the Single Market should lead to the development of a number of globally competitive EC firms and a restructuring of supplier relationships within the EC. North America's automotive industry is in a good position to take advantage of this changing market, particularly through joint ventures and technology sharing.

Increasing competitive pressures have made just-in-time systems and proximity to suppliers essential parts of competitive advantage in the sector. That means North American companies will need a real presence in the EC. Often, strategic alliances will be the only way to go. Joint ventures with accredited European suppliers can provide significantly increased market presence in the EC.

The heightened competition of the Single Market has made technology an even more important competitive ingredient for EC automotive firms. European firms will be on the lookout for companies that can supply product and process

Diagram 14   World Sales of New-Model Cars
(Millions of Cars)

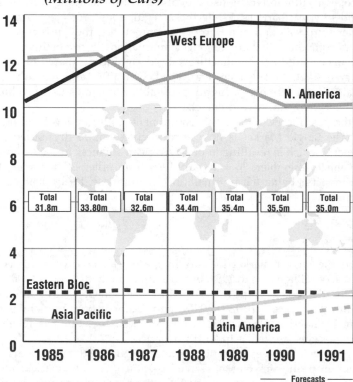

	Total	Total	Total	Total	Total	Total	Total
	31.8m	33.80m	32.6m	34.4m	35.4m	35.5m	35.0m

West Europe

N. America

Eastern Bloc

Asia Pacific

Latin America

1985   1986   1987   1988   1989   1990   1991

———— Forecasts ————

improvements. That means increased opportunities for innovative small and me-dium-sized North American automotive firms.

The automobile industries of North America, Japan, and the EC are approx-imately the same size: each produces about 12 million cars and trucks annually.

The European automotive industry is vital to EC prosperity. It accounts for about 9 percent of the industrial value-added content and employs 1.8 million people. Counting both direct and indirect employment (from suppliers to body shops), the industry employs one out of 10 workers in the EC. During the last half of the 1980s, the EC vehicle market experienced strong growth: from 1985 to 1988, the market grew from 10.8 million vehicles to 13.4 million vehicles, an increase of 24 percent.

EC companies have historically competed with each other, but they are now facing mounting pressure from world competitors, especially the Japanese.

Structure

The European automotive industry evolved within a framework of technical, fiscal, and physical barriers. While these regulations protected local producers from other European and non-European competitors, they also encouraged the survival of companies that are no longer internationally competitive.

Six major full-line manufacturers hold significant shares of the EC passenger car market: Volkswagen, Fiat, Ford, GM, PSA, and Renault. The Community also has a number of highly profitable companies that produce luxury cars: Daimler-Benz, BMW, and Porsche.

In the past the EC automotive components industry has been highly fragmented. The Single Market is now encouraging a more diversified pattern of procurement, which is resulting in pan-European alliances in the component sector. As vehicle assemblers look to suppliers from other EC member states, the greatest impact is being felt by small and medium-sized European components manufacturers.

Markets

The EC is the largest market for cars in the world. Five years of record sales peaked at 13.4 million cars in 1989, but growth came to an end in 1990 when new car sales fell 1.1 percent in the first 11 months. Sales in Germany continued to rise in 1990, but they were poor in the U.K. and Spain, as both economies went into recession. Demand has remained strong in Germany, but has fallen in other European markets, as well as in North America.

Commercial vehicles present a similar picture. After five years of record sales, the European truck market is in a downturn. German truck makers Daimler-Benz and MAN are doing very well, but the steep downturn in the UK and Spain has hit British and Spanish manufacturers hard.

European production of trucks with a gross weight above 3.5 tons was down 10.7 percent in the first eight months of 1990. The U.K., Spain, Sweden, and the Netherlands have been hit the hardest. With the continuing exception of Germany, EC truck sales were expected to keep dropping throughout 1992.

Outlook

Europe's automobile manufacturers may claim engineering and design leadership in some areas, but their overall competitiveness is poor by North American and Japanese standards. With the exception of luxury car builders who export to all parts of the world, sales by EC producers are generally restricted to European markets such as Spain, Italy, or France.

In the short term, the EC automotive industry is expected to suffer from the present recession. In the longer term, sales should pick up as a result of the emerging Single Market, rising demand from the East European market, and calls for environmental protection. Analysts are forecasting a much brighter picture for 1992 to 1995.

Biotechnology

The biotechnology sector in the EC, as in North America and Japan, is geared toward large firms that can bear the extremely high costs involved in R&D, testing, and marketing. While smaller firms play key roles in the industry, they tend to concentrate their activities on research for the traditional pharmaceutical industry and larger biotech firms. The typical biotech firm has strategic alliances with about six other companies, forming a complex network that serves to spread costs and risks while offering protection from takeover bids.

The quality of European R&D is widely recognized, and Europeans can rely on the vitality of several medium-sized, innovative firms backed by the funding capacities of the sector's major companies. Despite this, the European industry has been facing difficult problems, which the EC is now trying to redress.

Expansion into multiple EC national markets has been difficult due to the large variety of regulatory regimes and patent laws. This problem is being addressed through the development of predictable, pan-European standards, which should increase payoffs from the pan-European biotechnology R&D subsidies the EC is conducting.

The EC's income-support program for agricultural producers made the costs of fermentation feedstocks (starch, sugar) prohibitively high for a number of companies. In one example, a major application of enzyme technology (liquid sweetener) was commercialized in the U.S. rather than in the EC, even though many of the key developments that made it possible were European. This problem has been addressed through refunds, but it was a serious setback to the development of biotechnology in the EC.

Some observers estimate that because of such setbacks the European biotechnology industry is now three years behind Japan and North America. Europe has very likely lost its lead in molecular biotechnology, the U.S. dominates genetic engineering, and Japan is the world leader in advanced fermentation and separation technology.

Markets

The various applications of biotechnology have one thing in common: They all make use of living systems to carry out tasks or to make new products. Pharmaceuticals account for 68 percent of the biotechnology sector in the world, while food and agriculture make up another 24 percent.

Biotechnology has been used to improve livestock, plants, and fertilizer. The most frequent commercial applications in biotech areas are found in medical applications and plant genetics, however. While new therapeutic products have been slow to emerge, the most promising commercial area lies in the development of new diagnostic kits. The other commercially viable sector of medical biotechnology is the manufacture of vaccines and immunostimulants.

EC Programs

The BRIDGE Program (Biotechnology Research for Innovation, Development and Growth in Europe) covers information infrastructures (culture collections, data processing), enabling technologies (protein design, molecular modeling, gene mapping, biotransformation), cellular biology and pre-normative research (e.g., safety assessments and the evaluation of toxicity). Scheduled to run from 1990 to 1993, BRIDGE has a budget of $96 million.

Outlook

Because Europe lags behind somewhat in biotechnology, much of the trade-liberalizing consequences of the Single Market will benefit non-EC firms. Thus the principal competitors for North American firms entering the market will be Japanese.

This will be tough competition, but there are openings to be exploited, and a number of North American firms are already successfully taking advantage of them. Many North American firms have chosen to qualify as European companies by setting up a European subsidiary, either wholly owned, jointly owned with another North American company, or as a joint venture with a European firm.

Environmental Protection

The integration of the EC market presents a number of opportunities for North American firms in environmental services, and in certain niche-product markets, including water and wastewater treatment equipment, monitoring equipment, toxic waste disposal and air quality control.

The environmental services sector is a new and burgeoning industry. Attempts to estimate the size of the EC environmental protection industry have varied from $66.3 billion in 1987, to as much as $118.4 billion in 1989.

Although the industry itself is young, many of the firms involved in it are quite old. They come from such diverse sectors as mechanical engineering, chemistry, construction, instrumentation, and urban services. There are also a significant number of new companies: in Germany, for example, 49 percent of companies that enter the sector are new businesses.

Structure

The environmental industries of each member state vary a great deal. There are differences in concentration, vertical integration, public/private ownership, and areas of expertise.

With several thousand companies involved, the EC environmental protection industry is not highly concentrated. Many small and medium-sized businesses view the sector as a secondary area of activity. Deutsche Babcock, the largest of the German environmental firms, is an example of an equipment manufacturer diversifying into air and water pollution treatment and waste disposal. Engineering businesses that deal with water quality, emission treatment, the elimination of waste, and noise pollution are also in this core group.

There are a number of chemical, construction, and industrial giants gathered around this central group of businesses. While they are not heavily involved in the sector yet, their interest will probably grow in the future. In the meantime, many have started environmental divisions, including Focsa (Spain), Hozmann (Germany), Bouygues (France), and Wimpey (U.K.). Other major industrial groups involved in environmental technology include ASEA Brown Boveri and RWE (Rheinische Westfalische Elektrizitatswerke).

European firms are often active in non-EC markets. A French firm is in the number-one position in the field of water supply in North America, while a U.K. firm holds the number-four position in the collection and treatment of North American waste. At the same time, a number of non-EC firms are doing very well in the EC markets. For example, non-EC firms hold 80 percent of the market in environmental control instruments.

With the harmonization of EC environmental standards and the liberalization of public procurement in the EC, the industry is becoming more concentrated and more international. There has been a proliferation of alliances and M&As between EC firms, and numerous subsidiaries have been created. A large number of alliances with non-EC firms have also been formed. An example is the British-Canadian-U.S. group formed under Atwood and Laidlaw.

Markets

Environmental services markets often open in the wake of legislation, flourish for a few years, and then settle back to a subsistence level. As a result, the business is subject to short cycles, and few companies are able to focus exclusively on the sector or make long-term plans in it.

There are huge discrepancies between markets for environmental services in the different member states of the EC. The German market is larger than the French and the U.K. markets combined, and 50 to 100 times larger than the Greek, Irish, and Portuguese markets combined. These differences are caused by variations in population, industrial activity, and wealth, as well as by the differences between the environmental policies of the member states.

The most popular modes of EC market entry among non-EC environmental firms appear to be partnering or establishing a local office. There are a number of reasons for this. While strong demand will create many opportunities for North American environmental protection firms in the EC, Canadian and U.S. firms in this sector are likely to find that their strategic options are limited by a lack of qualified engineers.

Diagram 15   Agreements between European Environmental Firms, 1988–89

Companies	Type of Agreement	Area
Thames Water (U.K.)—Ansaldo (I)	Joint venture	Environmental management
Walther (FRG)—Alsthom (F)	Participation in a German firm	Emmission treatment stationary source
Kruger (DK)—Hölter (FRG)	Joint venture	Air and water treatment
DDS (DK)—Lyonnaise (F)	Cooperation in R&D	Water treatment
Biffa (U.K.)—Antward Waste Management (G)	Joint venture	Urban waste disposal
Italgas (I)—Générate des Eaux (F)	Joint venture	Water treatment
TNEE (F)—Deutsche Babcock (D)	Agreement/German licence	Emission treatment
Lyonnaise (F)—Fiat Engineering (I)	Joint venture	Water treatment
AIV (S)—Northumbrian Water (U.K.)	Joint venture	Water treatment

B= Belgium
S= Spain
U.K.= United Kingdom

FRG= Germany
F= France

DK= Denmark
I= Italy

Source: Recherche Development International

Exporting to the EC tends to work best in the small national markets or in the markets of southern Europe. For North American manufacturers of environmental goods, direct exports to the EC will be more feasible for high-value, low-volume goods. Otherwise, foreign manufacturers would likely be better off establishing a manufacturing presence in Europe, most often through licensing or partnering with European firms, rather than through greenfield investments or acquisitions, which tend to be more risky and expensive.

Acquisitions may make more sense for the larger environmental service companies. For example, Laidlaw acquired Atwoods, a U.K. waste management firm, while SAUR (a unit of the Bouygues conglomerate in France) bought a part of two Spanish firms. Even then, however, many of these purchases involve a minority position and often preserve the local character and ownership of the firm, an important consideration in public-sector contracts.

Programs

The development of new technologies plays an important part in the sector, affecting areas as diverse as mechanical and chemical procedures and filtering, to advanced biotechnological methods and lasers. Because of the uncertainty and short life span of environmental markets, medium- and long-term R&D by the EC private sector has tended to lag. In order to overcome this, some EC countries are spending a good deal of money—especially Germany, which in 1985 spent more on R&D in this sector than the US and all the other EC countries combined.

ENVIREG is an EC program that supports larger-scale environmental projects in the poorer regions of the EC. ENVIREG funding for projects complements aid provided by regional governments. Companies cannot apply directly to the program, but must work through the regional governments.

While ENVIREG provides larger-scale regional aid, MEDSPA (Community Action for the Protection of the Environment in the Mediterranean Basin) provides venture capital funding. Proposed projects must offer innovative solutions to environmental problems, and other communities must also benefit from them. Total funding for the project is modest: $11 million in 1990, $16 million in 1991, and $18 million in 1992.

European companies must apply directly to the Commission, while North American firms would have to get the support of the regional or provincial government where the project is located.

The Network for Environmental Technology Transfer (NETT) is an EC-sponsored database which provides information on suppliers of environmental protection technologies. Hundreds of firms of all sizes and from all environmental sectors have been listed. Non-EC companies can be listed at a higher fee.

Under the Environmental Program for the Mediterranean, the World Bank and the European Investment Bank (EIB) assist projects aimed at protecting the Mediterranean Sea. Support is provided for project design and implementation, institution building, policy advice and formulation, and the mobilization of financial resources. There are four priority areas: integrated water resource management, management of hazardous wastes, prevention and control of marine pollution from oil and chemicals, and coastal zone management. Half of the EIB's environmental spending since 1980 has gone into the program, amounting to almost $3.3 billion. The World Bank spent $2.3 billion over the same period.

REWARD (Recycling Waste Research & Development) is an EC program designed to increase recycling, alleviate problems of waste disposal and environmental pollution, and improve the management of raw materials and energy resources. The program is scheduled to run from 1990 to 1992 with a budget of $9 million. It is open to all universities, higher education institutes, research organizations, and industrial enterprises established in the member states.

REWARD is also open to international organizations and to enterprises from nonmember states that, through an appropriate agreement, are partly or wholly associated with it. Proposals must specify the location where the various parts of the R&D are to be carried out.

In July 1988, 14 Eureka environmental projects were launched involving 78 participants, at a total estimated cost of $580.4 million. A framework program for the development of technology projects was set in motion in 1989.

Outlook

The prospects of the European environmental sector are vast because of increasing public demand for a healthier environment, expanding demand in other parts of the world, and the ongoing demand for operation and maintenance service on an increasing capital stock of environmental protection equipment. Because demand is tied to political decisions, the medium-term view is uncertain. Over the longer term, however, European environmental services is a sector with a promising future.

Financial Services

EC markets present a variety of opportunities for North American financial institutions. There is a growing demand in Europe for more sophisticated financial products, and the offerings of U.S. and Canadian firms are state-of-the-art.

Financial services in the EC have been growing steadily, both in terms of the number of people the sector employs and in terms of value added to the economy. However, this share varies enormously from country to country—from 4 percent of France's value-added in the total GDP, to almost 15 percent of Luxembourg's value-added. The particularly high share of the financial services in the economies of Luxembourg and the U.K. is due to the international character of their financial markets. London is still the financial center of Europe.

Despite the rapid expansion of the financial sector in Europe, it is still not as developed as in other industrialized regions. For example, in 1987 the share of stock market capitalization in the EC was 21 percent, as opposed to 33 percent in the U.S. and 42 percent in Japan.

Structure

Privatization is the trend in an EC banking sector already dominated by the private sector. Public-sector banks tend to specialize in areas such as supplying longer-term investment financing.

At present, banking accounts for 65 percent of the employment in financial services, but increasing competition and concentration in banking will eventually lead to fewer jobs in this subsector.

The insurance industry is an important part of the financial services sector. In 1987, the value of gross premiums received by insurers totalled $339.6 billion, or about 5.5 percent of European GDP. The industry employs approximately 1.2 million people.

The insurance industry experienced a high rate of growth between 1960 and 1980, but in the face of North American and Japanese expansion in the 1980s, its market share fell from more than 27 percent of the world market to less than 23 percent. Still, annual rates of increase within the EC have remained high.

EC countries are developing a common market in the financial services sector in progressive stages. Capital flows, banking, and insurance services and the stocks and bonds market are being liberalized.

This process is leading to a diversification of activities both for banks and insurance companies. For example, banks are selling insurance policies of affiliated insurance companies, while insurance companies are dealing in pension funds. As a result, the differences between various types of institutions are becoming blurred. It is thought that banks will try to use technology to create a barrier to competition from institutions that are not banks.

A pattern of loose confederations is emerging in the European financial services sector. In general, institutions have found that strategic alliances are more flexible tools than mergers. Alliances between banks and insurance companies are common, especially in Germany.

Banking and Insurance Alliances in the EC

A classic example of a European banking and insurance partnership is the cooperation agreement which the Banque Indosuez signed with View Rotterdam in the Netherlands and with Baltica Holdings, a Danish insurance and finance company. The deal enabled Banque Indosuez to add Scandinavia to its EC-wide networks, while the smaller Baltica Holdings can now offer its Danish corporate clients access to a pan-European network. The deal will also provide Baltica Holdings with improved access to capital markets, allowing it to grow as a specialized Danish merchant bank. And it provides Baltica with new capital and protection against a hostile takeover.

There is significant investment in new technology as institutions try to increase productivity and reduce costs. The banking sector is dominating the development of EFTPOS (Electronic funds transfer at the point of sale). Retailing organizations expect to hold a 25 percent share of EFTPOS networks by 1995. Credit-card companies and savings/mortgage institutions are expected to be major players. More than half of all retail customers are likely to use the network.

Markets

Rather than providing global banking services, North American banks in the EC are focusing on high-caliber niche products, as well as providing their international corporate clients with key services. Service is provided by small teams of highly skilled and mobile specialists operating from a central base, usually London.

U.S. and Canadian brokerage houses that establish in Europe will find a good market for their equities and bonds. Properly promoted, the thorough research capabilities of the North American securities industry should find a receptive market in Europe.

North Americans can also offer sophisticated experience in the management of mutual funds. France, Luxembourg, and the U.K. contain many funds, while Italy and Spain are becoming large markets for foreign mutuals since local funds cannot keep up with the demand.

There is a large and growing demand for insurance and pension products. While most EC member states have comprehensive social security systems, there is a concern that these systems may not provide an adequate level of protection. The markets with the most potential are Italy and Spain, where the demand for insurance products is expected to grow by 20 to 30 percent for the next five years. France also looks very promising.

Insurance markets vary greatly from country to country. The largest national markets are Germany, the U.K., and France. The lowest proportions of life insurance to total business were in Portugal, Spain, and Italy.

Insurance markets in the EC are fairly concentrated. In life insurance, ten leading companies share more than 80 percent of the market. In only one EC country is the market share of the top ten below 50 percent. The markets for non-life insurance are less concentrated. In two EC countries, the ten largest firms write more than 80 percent of the business, whereas in five other EC countries the share of the leading 10 companies is below 50 percent.

While North American insurance companies may lack comprehensive distribution networks in the EC, they have the kind of sophisticated services in life

A Comparison of Financial Markets (in percent)

Insurance[1]

EC	21.60
U.S.	45.50
Japan	19.80

Stock Market[2]

EC	27.64
U.S.	47.70
Japan	114.30

Banking[3]

EC	33.30
U.S.	14.50
Japan	36.40

Source: Eurostat, DRI Europe.
1. Insurance market share per head (1986)
2. Stock market capitalization as % GDP (1987)
3. Bank share of consolidated international claims (1987)

insurance and pension products that EC companies are looking for—an excellent basis for mutually advantageous alliances.

Programs

The Venture Capital Consortia pilot system is aimed at encouraging the growth of European SMEs through the formation of cross-border syndicates of venture capital companies.

The EC is participating in the project as a sponsoring and funding agency, providing support in the form of non-interest-bearing grants to be converted into equity by the lead investor, within certain limits. The EC will supply 30 percent of the syndicate's equity investments by full members of the European Venture Capital Association (EVCA), but not less than $74,300 and not more than $445,800.

The objective of the Venture Capital Consortia is to create a Europe-wide market for venture capital investments. Since its launch, the Commission of the European Communities (CEC) has approved 35 venture consort projects for a total contribution of $8.05 million.

Firms wishing to take advantage of this program should conform to the following procedures:

- At least two different companies established in the Community prepare an investment proposal and submit it to venture capital firms.

- Once it has agreed to invest in the project, the lead investor sends the application to the European Venture Capital Association office, which checks it and forwards it to the CEC.

- The CEC informs EVCA and the lead investor as to whether it will contribute to the financing or not.

The Commission's contract is with the lead investor. Applications take a maximum of four to five months to approve.

Outlook

The integration of the EC financial services market will have a profound effect on the whole economy. Investors will be able to access a broader range of financial instruments and diversify their portfolios. The resulting capital flows will also have the effect of leveling off interest rates, improving profit margins, and therefore improving the efficiency of capital throughout the EC.

Given the sophistication of the North American financial sector, companies that make their move now should be able to find solid European partners, but this will become increasingly difficult as EC firms position themselves within the Single Market.

Food and Drink

European food and drink companies are buying and selling each other and forming new alliances at record rates. Some firms are raising huge amounts of capital in order to buy other companies, while others are eager to sell off unwanted plants. The process is part of a global movement toward internationalization of the industry in response to exchange rate and raw material fluctuations.

Two types of groups are emerging: conglomerates with diversified holdings such as Hillsdown Holdings, Hanson and Beatrice (BCI Holdings), and more specialized or focused groups such as BSN, Ferruzzi, RJR Nabisco, and Phillip Morris.

Europe has the two largest food and drink companies in the world, Unilever and Nestlé. The next eight corporations among the top ten, however, are American. With the exception of the largest firms, EC companies do not seem to have developed Single Market strategies, and US firms are thought to be better placed to exploit emerging Single Market opportunities.

The food and drink industry in the EC contains a great variety of sectors, firms, and business practices. It tends to be more concentrated in northern Europe. Rationalization has begun in Italy, Spain, and Portugal, but the industry in those countries is still highly fragmented and vulnerable to the giant food groups of the north.

Markets

European tastes are moving toward more elaborately processed food, and products with a higher technological and service element. Three types of products are becoming increasingly important:

- higher-quality products such as low-fat milk, fresh poultry, high-fiber products, whole-wheat bread, and products with fewer additives;

- higher-convenience products such as breakfast cereals and meals that can be quickly heated in the microwave;

- high-variety products such as fresh juices and exotic fruits.

Many firms are exploring improved methods of modified atmosphere packaging, a new technology that uses nitrogen and carbon gases to preserve fruits, vegetables, and bakery goods in sealed containers.

The strategies being used by North American food and beverage firms in the EC tend to depend on their size. Many of the large ones are creating new firms or acquiring existing EC companies. For small and medium-sized firms, responding to Single Market opportunities more often involves finding a good sales agent or alliance partner, improving productivity, and adopting international standards.

EC Programs

European Collaborative Linkage of Agriculture and Industry through Research (ECLAIR) promotes useful applications of recent developments in the life sciences and biotechnology. Scheduled to last from 1988 to 1993, it has a budget of $112.9 million.

Food Linked Agro-Industrial Research (FLAIR) focuses on the interface between consumer, industry, and research. It concentrates on the downstream end of food science and technology that emphasizes the measurement and enhancement of food quality, food hygiene, safety and toxicology, nutrition and wholesome aspects. FLAIR is scheduled from 1989 to 1993, with a budget of $35 million.

Outlook

A 1988 EC report identified more than 200 nontariff barriers between EC countries, which together cost the industry $145.1 million to $725.5 million annually. These barriers often apply to trade in food and agriculture products. They consist mostly of packaging and labeling regulations, specific import restrictions (e.g., sanitary laws in the U.K. or Spain), and content or denomination regulations (e.g., for beer).

The elimination of nontariff barriers will allow companies to buy less expensive ingredients, reduce their packaging and labeling costs, and eliminate bureaucratic and administrative restrictions of imports. It has been estimated that their elimination will save 2 to 3 percent of the sector's total value-added. Sector areas that will benefit the most are oils and fats, chocolate, ice cream, pasta, saccharine, beer, and plastic containers.

Information Technologies

North American information technology companies have developed impressive global markets, and are well positioned to take advantage of changes arising out of the Single Market.

Information technology is a vast and rapidly evolving industry that encompasses computers, telecommunications, microelectronics, instrumentation, electric components, and software. With the growing integration of voice, data, and visual communications, these areas are becoming hard to distinguish. They have given rise to a variety of telecommunications services such as mobile telephones, new broadcasting technologies, facsimile, videotext, telex, packet and circuit-switched data.

The EC produces almost a quarter of the world's computer and electronic goods. Electronics production represents 8 percent of overall industrial production in the EC, and has been one of its fastest growing sectors. Between 1980 and 1988, telecommunications and audiovisual equipment grew at a rate of 9 percent annually, while computers and office equipment grew at 14 percent.

Structure

Global information technology is a highly concentrated industry. For example, in telecommunications, the ten largest companies control about half of the market.

The EC sector is likewise dominated by large firms. The two largest EC companies, Siemens and Philips, are industry heavyweights. Philips is the seventh largest company in the EC. In 1988, its worldwide turnover reached $34.8 billion, 61 percent of which was generated in Europe.

Competition has led to increasing internationalization in the technology sector. In order to survive, European firms have had to establish themselves in the US market. This, added to the astronomical costs and risks involved in the development of new products, has stimulated M&As and strategic alliances both at home and abroad.

R&D Costs Drive Alliances and M&As

Although Nixdorf started to penetrate the U.S. market successfully in the late 1980s, it had to be acquired by Siemens in order to remain healthy. Conversely, CGE and ITT concluded an agreement that enabled CGE to increase its presence in different EC countries, and to a lesser degree in the US. In order to keep up with internationalization, ICL of the U.K. was acquired by Fujitsu of Japan.

The public sector is a dominant force in the telecommunications and electronic information services sectors, although this is changing with Community-wide liberalization. The current trend is toward privatization. British Telecom, for example, was privatized in 1984, and has given regulatory and supervisory authority to a private company, Oftel.

Developing Europe's telecommunications infrastructure is essential to achieving the full benefits of the Single Market. The waste and lack of competition associated with the fragmentation of public procurement in the Community is estimated to cost approximately $30 billion per year. With this in mind, in June 1987 the EC Commission issued a Green Paper on telecommunications, containing a program of regulatory change to meet the twin challenges of 1992 and technological development.

As a result, public procurement has been opened for all value-added services within and between member states, and the movement of terminal equipment and receiving antenna equipment within and between member states has been liberalized. Any measure that prevents the movement of goods between member countries has been prohibited. Barriers to imports and legislation that could indirectly have the same effect have also been prohibited.

It is no longer possible, for example, to require that certain products conform to standards that only national manufacturers could meet. Restrictions that discriminate against non-nationals seeking to establish professional activities in EC countries have also been prohibited.

These measures also seek to ensure the publication of tender notices and to prohibit the illegal exclusion of bidders or applicants from member states. Provisions to this effect are expected to be fully implemented by 1994.

The few European companies still committed to microchip production have placed their faith in JESSI—the $5 billion Joint European Submicron Silicon research initiative.

JESSI has encountered problems, however. Philips has cut its commitment to the program, while U.S. and Japanese firms established as manufacturers in the

EC are demanding the right to participate in it. The newly arrived U.S. and Japanese players include Texas Instruments, which is building a factory in the U.K., and Hitachi and Mitsubishi, which are setting up in Germany.

Information technologies tend to be very concentrated, but this is not the case for computer software. There are 13,000 to 15,000 EC software companies, employing 287,000 people.

The diverse products and services in this sector are supplied by a variety of companies, including hardware manufacturers who sell software, systems houses, independent software vendors, professional consultancies, computing centers, software training specialists, and business information services.

The sector has developed differently in the various member states. Software packaging is stronger in Germany, while custom software and consulting is more highly developed in France.

Market

The importance of information technologies to the EC member states varies considerably. Because of non-EC investment in production facilities, for example, information technologies accounted for 17 percent of Irish industrial production in 1988, but only 5 percent of Italy's industrial production, and 3 percent of Spain's.

New product prices are initially very high, as the product development company attempts to recoup its R&D investment. Prices then fall to discourage other competitors. European companies tend to enter the market late, after the price has fallen, and for this reason they often have a hard time paying back their investment.

In the telecommunications industry, the financial stakes are considerable, since the EC market accounts for almost a quarter of the total world market. North America has a well-developed telecommunications industry, and the strengths necessary to do well in the EC. The success of smaller firms will depend on their ability to identify and fill market niches in the EC.

Worldwide, computer services and software have been the fastest growing areas in information technologies. This is particularly true in Europe, where sales have been driven by the integration of European markets. In fact, European sales have been major factors in keeping the North American industry afloat. For example, in 1989, 71 percent of IBM's net income came from Europe, making up for its losses in the U.S. market. As a result, the world's computer companies are scrambling to position themselves in Europe.

Many North American service firms have followed their large customer firms into international markets. The decision by the Commission of the EC to adopt integrated services digital network (ISDN) as the basis of a future EC telecommunications-information network also opens up numerous opportunities for new software and integrated systems development.

EC Policy and Programs

The two major EC programs for information technologies are RACE and ESPRIT. Their combined five-year budgets are $3.2 billion. When the matching private sector contributions are included, the two programs involve $6.4 billion.

The main thrust of the RACE initiative is to develop the next generation in telecommunications infrastructure. It has also sought to develop and harmonize standards for an ISDN, digital mobile communications, and future broadband communications. And it is promoting Europe-wide open standards for terminals and equipment.

ESPRIT is focusing on microelectronics technologies. Its projects involve transnational cooperative ventures that include firms and government as well as academic research labs.

EFTA countries have been granted limited involvement in a number of the EC technological programs. Whether non-European firms will be eligible for ESPRIT or RACE grants is not altogether clear, but the minimum eligibility criteria require having an EC subsidiary or subcontracting to an EC consortium member.

Outlook

In 1990, dramatic changes in costs and technology drove marketing costs skyward, while demand for information technology products in Europe and the U.S. declined as a result of recessions in the U.K. and the U.S., and because large customers were trying to cut back on the amount they spent on information technology.

In the future, the sectors most likely to do well are personal computers, particularly laptops, and those technologies that can improve the productivity of existing systems. The computer industry is looking to a combination of new software, new markets, and lower prices to regain customers.

Many information technology suppliers are seeking new and more profitable ventures. There is a good deal of potential in ISDN and high-definition television, for example.

Opportunities for North American firms in the EC are more likely to take the form of an established presence rather than arms-length trading. For larger firms this may mean acquisitions or greenfield investments, while small and medium-sized firms will have to develop multinational capabilities if they want to address an EC-wide market. For many, strategic alliances will be the most economical route.

CHAPTER 11

FINANCING YOUR ENTRY INTO THE EC

- ALLIANCE STRUCTURE
- ROLES OF PARTIES
- CAPITAL SOURCES AVAILABLE
- TAXATION AND LEGAL ASPECTS
- RISKS AND REWARDS
- STATEMENTS OF FINANCIAL CRITERIA

The following factors are important in determining how your strategic alliance should be financed. These factors should not be considered in isolation; they are interconnected, and the decision on the form and amount of financing should be made based on how each factor influences the overall deal.

The Structure of the Alliance

The type of strategic alliance contemplated will influence the extent and nature of the financial commitment to the alliance. For instance, a joint venture based on equal shares for the partners will have different financing implications than would a licensing arrangement or a marketing agreement.

Joint ventures involve more significant legal and financial obligations than do other forms of cooperation. In fact, co-marketing, cross-manufacturing and cross-licensing alliances may not require much financial commitment at all, since they involve the use of existing resources that can be financed out of existing operating budgets.

Roles of Parties

The amount that a company may be willing to invest in an alliance will depend on its role. It may assume the role of financier, in which case it takes on the responsibility for providing capital for the whole project. If it wants controlling interest in a project, it will almost always have to make a corresponding financial contribution.

Sometimes an investment is required as evidence of serious interest in and commitment to a project. In other cases, financing may be limited to an initial exploration of future possibilities for cooperation.

If the role of one of the parties is to contribute know-how to a project, it may offer rights to a patent in exchange for shares in the venture. This kind of transaction may be especially advantageous when the country in which the transfer is made taxes dividends from shares at lower rates than it does royalties from patents.

Capital Sources Available

Much also depends on the availability of local financing. North American companies may discover sources of reasonably priced capital in any EC country or regions. Regional governments and their institutions can be particularly helpful in providing access to local sources of financing (see Chapter 5).

Private institutions such as banks and suppliers may view an alliance as an attractive business opportunity representing reasonable risk for the returns involved. Guarantees may also be offered by one of the parties, in order to help the venture obtain financing at reasonable rates, without committing the internal funds of either partner. Given the strength and reputation of either party, a stock issue may be possible in the country targeted for investment.

International lending institutions, such as the European Investment Bank (EIB), may have an interest in participating financially in the venture because it may complement their mandate or their other interests. For example, through its New Community Instrument IV, the EC works with the EIB to raise capital for small and medium-sized businesses.

Taxation and Legal Aspects

Tax laws vary on the issue of residency and control. Who controls a company and where it resides often has a bearing on the corporate taxes the alliance would pay, and in which country.

The objective of tax treaties is to prevent double taxation, to establish fiscal cooperation between taxing authorities of the signatory countries, to ensure fairness to taxpayers, and to provide for adequate enforcement of respective revenue laws.

Such treaties tend to reduce the amount of tax that a corporation from one country must pay another country. Thus, in setting up the alliance, it is important to consider how one can best take advantage of the various tax treaties that exist in North America and throughout Europe. Proper planning can greatly reduce one's tax burden.

Risks and Rewards

The potential financial return on a given strategic alliance, proportional to risk involved, may represent an opportunity that cannot be matched by other available investment opportunities such as the money markets or other business projects. In such a situation, if funds are available, it may be desirable for the company to assume financial responsibility for the largest part of the investment.

Statements of Financial Criteria

Your firm should formulate criteria that enable you to define financial performance objectives, policies relating to investments, financing risk, new share issues, retained earnings, and earnings-per-share targets. This statement should also include your intentions in terms of funding requirements, sources of funds, key financial ratios and dividend objectives. Finally, it should describe the organization and structure you will use to manage the financial affairs of the proposed venture.

Checklist for Financing a Strategic Alliance

It would be difficult to provide a list that covers aspects relevant to all the possible forms of alliance. The following checklist is a starting point for determining what you will need.

1. Is the return on the investment employed for the alliance commensurate with the risks involved?

2. What is the financial capacity of your potential foreign partners? Consider the extent and nature of their possible financial commitment, as well as other possible forms of participation.

3. What banking facilities are available? What is the nature of the credit facilities offered? This includes short-, medium-, and long-term (conditions, terms, interest rates, etc.) from domestic, foreign, government, and other lending institutions and facilities.

4. What loans are available?

5. What funds or other resources are available from third-country operations?

6. What accounting and legal services are available in your potential partner's home jurisdiction?

7. What currencies, exchange rates, and controls on capital flows and remittances are involved? How stable is the currency?

8. What is involved in the repatriation of capital, licensing fees, and other payments?

9. Are the tax policies stable and equitable? How will domestic and foreign taxation affect the formation, operation, and disposition or repatriation of funds and remittance of profits?

10. Is insurance available to cover non-business risks, such as expropriation, convertibility, and civil strife?

11. What is the value of the know-how, technology, or other intellectual property being contributed to the alliance?

12. What level of management control would be commensurate with the investment required?

13. *Do you have optimum freedom to re-invest in the jurisdiction of the alliance to expand, develop technology, or improve quality?*

Sources: U.S. Department of Commerce, Bureau of International Commerce, Office of International Investment, Washington, DC, and R. Duane Hall, Ph.D., International Joint Venture (1984).

Financial Criteria

- the method you will use to finance new investment;

- the cost and timing of new plant, personnel, and inventory requirements;

- the timing of additional revenues likely to be accrued against new working capital requirement;

- terms to be negotiated with debtors and creditors;

- banking arrangements to be negotiated in new markets;

- requirements to deal with foreign currency and transactions of existing markets;

- new sources of business financing and their costs, including overseas banking.

CHAPTER 12

WORKING WITHIN A DIFFERENT CULTURE

- ## CULTURAL BARRIERS
- ## EC FUTURE

Cultural Barriers

Successful management of a strategic alliance goes beyond overcoming organizational challenges. It also involves dealing with the peculiarities of European social and corporate practices. These cultural differences can pose major stumbling blocks for North American firms seeking to build EC alliances. Success often depends on the quality and the skills of the people involved, especially the general manager.

Finding the right person to run the strategic alliance—or to look after the liaison points between the partners—is of vital importance. Such people must have enough power to make things happen, and they must have a good understanding of the respective cultures and practices of the parent companies. They should be thoroughly competent in their normal managerial or technical roles and they will need strong interpersonal skills. They must be active listeners, able to sense the unspoken and hidden dynamics of the other side and find reasonable compromises.

You will also want to share your company's business objectives in the EC with your employees at all levels. Their cooperation with EC counterparts will be vital.

And your European personnel may need guidance on how to obtain information and help from their North American counterparts. Prepare written guidelines from both operations, and include clear directions, names, job functions, and phone numbers. Otherwise, simple details such as time-zone differences can become major problems. Remember to take the time to keep the lines of communication open.

Entering European markets involves learning a whole new set of skills. Carefully assess the linguistic skills of your employees, their familiarity and openness toward other cultures, and their attitudes toward the new business challenge. Your people may also need to develop new skills in marketing, distribution, export and import procedures, and quality and stock control. Once you have identified what new skills your managers and workers need, you will want to consider how they can be provided through:

- in-house training

- new recruitment

- educational institutions

- external training

- staff incentives

- correspondence courses

Some companies have launched special efforts to prepare their managers for strategic alliance management. Honeywell Europe, for example, has an intensive program to teach several hundred managers about European culture, values, and ethics. There are many consultants who can help firms customize training programs. Smaller firms that may not be able to afford such services could consider pooling their resources to organize the training they need.

Educational institutions have also developed training programs. The Ontario Centre of International Business at York University offers an enhanced MBA program, the first of its kind in Canada. It requires students to learn one foreign language, study other cultures, and spend one work term in another country.

A number of schools across Europe are forming joint programs in order to train future and present business leaders for the new European environment. Two recent examples of such cooperative initiatives at the graduate level are the European Business School (EAP), which has branches in France and Germany, and the joint venture between Ashridge Management College (UK), CPA (France), and USW (Germany).

The Good International Manager

Phillippe Gras, CEO of Renault Vehicles Industriels Group in Boulogne, lists several characteristics that Renault considers especially important in a European manager:

- the knowledge of several foreign languages, spoken fluently, enabling cultures, mentalities, and the history of several countries to be integrated.

- capacity to feel at ease in Barcelona or Frankfurt—to assure identical efficiency in several European countries. That inevitably implies experience abroad.

- high ideals—necessary for making comparative judgment so as not to reproduce identical models in countries where cultures are different.

In France, the European Business School Program, located at the Ecole des Hautes Etudes Commerciales, offers places to North Americans. Another French institution, CEDEP, is a continuing management education center linked to IN-SEAD.

INSEAD: Preparing a New Generation of Euro-Managers

INSEAD, a European business school modeled after the Harvard Business School, has developed a variety of courses for the new generation of Euro-managers. In addition to a normal MBA program, the continuing management education program draws more than 2,500 business executives to Fontainebleau each year. Courses there use the case method and are taught by an international faculty in English.

Courses normally run from two to six weeks. They include:

- *"Managing Partnerships and Strategic Alliances" (one week),*

- *"European Marketing Program" (three weeks), and*

- *"Managerial Skills for International Business" (two weeks).*

INSEAD also offers a two-week course in "Managing Multinational Enterprise." Topics covered include: the evolution of international competition, strategic options for multinationals, alternative strategies for penetration and disengagement, how to analyze political risks, and the influence of the social context. Cases studied include Michelin, Caterpillar, Komatsu, Heineken, Bok Paints, Triton Chemicals, Procter & Gamble, as well as international M&As (Electrolux-Zanussi), partnerships, and alliances.

INSEAD is very much a European school with an international "student" body. In 1990, 17 percent of the participants in their programs were from the UK, 14 percent from France, 11 percent from Germany, 11 percent from Scandinavia, 31 percent from other European countries, 8 percent from the Americas, 5 percent from the Pacific Rim and 3 percent from the rest of the world.

EC FUTURE

While short-term prospects for the EC economy are less favorable than they appeared in 1991, the fundamentals remain healthy. The U.K. and Spain are now in recession, and the German economy is showing signs of slowdown ahead. But other EC economies such as France and Italy are growing, although more slowly than in previous years.

In 1990, the EC's GDP is estimated to have increased by about 3 percent in real terms. In 1991, EC economic growth slowed to about 2.25 percent. This slowing is due to internal factors that were aggravated by the Persian Gulf War, the depreciation of the dollar, and current problems in the U.S. economy.

Employment is still growing, but growth slowed in 1991. Because EC currencies have been appreciating in value relative to other currencies, the EC has not been hit as hard as other economies by the inflationary effects of oil price increases. Nevertheless, inflation is increasing.

Longer-term prospects look positive. The EC has a solid industrial infrastructure and the achievement of a single internal market will provide an extra boost. Opportunities for companies in R&D should expand as government, private industry, and the European Commission encourage a wide range of cooperative research programs.

There should also be opportunities in public procurement—which represents about 16 percent of the EC's GDP—particularly for those North American firms that are subcontracting or partnering with EC firms. Once the dust settles, German unification is expected to have a positive effect, and companies in the EC will also be able to take advantage of new East European markets.

Liberalization and harmonization of the EC markets, and increasing European cooperation, is creating new opportunities in a number of emerging industrial sectors, especially telecommunications, pharmaceuticals, civil aerospace, and the food and beverage industry.

It should also be remembered that in difficult economic times, international competitive pressures only increase. More than ever, corporations need to spread their markets over North America, Europe, and Asia.

Expensive strategies such as acquisitions and greenfield investment will become more difficult to sustain. Strategic alliances, on the other hand, offer less expensive ways to expand into important markets such as the EC.

GDP at Constant Prices (percent change)

	1988	1989	1990	1991	1992
Canada	4.4	3.0	0.9	−0.3	3.6
Belgium	4.3	4.0	3.5	2.3	2.8
Denmark	−0.4	1.3	0.9	1.0	1.8
Greece	4.0	2.6	1.2	1.0	1.5
France	3.3	3.6	2.5	2.5	2.8
Germany	3.7	3.3	4.3	3.3	2.0
Ireland	3.7	5.9	4.5	2.3	3.8
Italy	3.9	3.2	2.6	2.3	2.8
Luxembourg	4.3	6.1	3.2	3.0	3.3
Netherlands	2.7	4.0	3.4	2.0	2.5
Portugal	3.9	5.4	4.2	3.3	3.8
Spain	5.0	4.9	3.5	2.5	3.3
U.K/	4.1	2.2	1.5	0.8	2.5
U.S.	4.6	2.5	1.1	0.3	1.3
Japan	5.7	4.9	6.0	4.3	4.0

Source: EC Annual Economic Report 1990 and Conference Board of Canada.

PART III

THE ASIA-PACIFIC REGION

CHAPTER 13

ASIA-PACIFIC OPPORTUNITIES

- **FIVE COUNTRIES, FIVE OPPORTUNITIES**
- **SETTING THE PACE**

Countries of Opportunity

North American companies seeking Asia-Pacific alliance partners should focus their efforts on five countries: Japan, Korea, Singapore, Taiwan, and Australia.

These countries share a number of reasons for pursuing overseas partnerships, including a wariness of undue dependence on export markets, a growing importance of investment versus trade, a need to cushion the impact of rapid export-led growth, and a hunger for new technology. But each country also has highly specific motives, and these must be understood by any company looking for alliance partners in the Asia-Pacific region.

Accordingly, this section of **The Asia-Pacific Region** has been divided into chapters examining the economic, political, and cultural characteristics of each country on an individual basis. Because North American businesses often find themselves navigating unfamiliar commercial waters when they venture into the Asia-Pacific region, background information is provided on the economic history, status, future goals, and strategy of each country.

Each chapter also contains information on business etiquette, designed to familiarize Western companies with the unique, unwritten rules of Asian business practice. The section closes with some final guidelines on doing business in the Asia-Pacific region.

Setting the Pace

The Asia-Pacific region has great potential for North American companies seeking alliance partners. It boasts some of the world's most powerful and rapidly advancing economies, which, like the EC member states, are moving to consolidate their strengths into a unified trading bloc.

The Pacific Rim has not yet achieved the cohesion of the European Economic Community, or Single Market clout, but it is undoubtedly moving in that direction. And the individual strengths of Asia-Pacific countries match, or surpass, anything Europe has to offer. Japan has been a world economic and technological giant for decades, while several other countries in the region are quickly becoming influential forces in the global marketplace.

In addition, the competitive drive of the Asia-Pacific countries is unmatched anywhere in the world. Japan must continue pursuing and adapting its aggressive export and investment strategies if it hopes to face increasing competition from its Pacific Rim neighbors, as well from the newly formed EC and North American trading blocs.

The region's developing economies—South Korea, Singapore, Taiwan, and Australia—require foreign technology, resources, and markets in order to make the leap from regional to global economic powers. In order to meet these competitive challenges, Pacific Rim nations are increasingly turning to strategic alliances.

Alliances are seen as especially useful tools for gaining access to new technology. All the countries featured in this chapter have recognized the importance of technology, and have invested heavily in it. In this they have followed the lead of Japan, which was the first country in the region to climb the technology ladder, moving from low-cost production into knowledge-intensive industries.

Today, Japan is characterized by the innovative application of existing technologies, coupled with an ambitious focus on basic research. In just two years, from 1986 to 1988, Japan's total public and private sector investment in R&D increased by almost a third, from approximately $97.3 billion to $115.6 billion.

Following Japan's example, South Korea, Taiwan, and Singapore have also made their way up the technology ladder. They have mastered light manufacturing and are beginning to move into more advanced industrial technologies. They also want to free themselves from undue dependence on Japanese technology. For example, between 1986 and 1988, South Korea's investment in R&D increased by 23 percent.

Because they recognize the importance of technology to economic growth, Asia-Pacific companies are looking to overseas partnerships to supplement their domestic technologies. Even the traditionally resource-based Australian economy is on the look-out for new technology. Today, Australians are attempting to refocus their economic activities on more value-added and knowledge-intensive sectors, and there is much that can be done through North American partnerships to move in this direction.

Asia-Pacific countries have an additional reason for entering into strategic alliances. The region currently enjoys a considerable stock of surplus capital, acquired as a result of an emphasis on export-oriented growth. Many Western countries are now deeply concerned about imbalances in their trade with the region, and, increasingly, this concern is manifesting itself in the form of import quotas and other trade barriers.

For this reason, more and more Pacific Rim companies are turning to investment as the preferred vehicle for penetrating international markets—and strategic alliances as the preferred vehicle for investment.

In fact, it is fair to say that investment has overtaken export as the driving force behind the world's great economies. And because Asia-Pacific companies have an impressive store of wealth accumulated from previous export drives, the pursuit of international investment opportunities is a strategy they can now well afford.

There are other reasons for the successful exporting countries of the Asia-Pacific region to pursue overseas alliances. Some are concerned that a rapid repatriation of profits earned from exports would fuel domestic inflation, perhaps provoking an abrupt and unwanted restructuring of their economies.

Therefore, investment in overseas alliances is not only a way for companies to maintain economic growth, but a means of cushioning the effects of rapid growth on their domestic economies, giving these economies time to adapt.

North American companies should be ready to take advantage of the willingness of their Asia-Pacific counterparts to enter into strategic alliances. The region is rich in technology, manufacturing know-how, labor and specialized markets—resources not found anywhere else in the world. In particular, the premium placed on research and development throughout the Asia-Pacific region, and the expertise in commercializing technology and streamlining production, are priceless commodities to U.S. and Canadian firms hoping to compete in an increasingly competitive global marketplace.

General Motors Succeeds With Japanese Know-how

Adam Opel AG is a wholly-owned General Motors subsidiary making cars in Germany for the European market. By 1993, a new $645 million Opel plant will become the first GM operation in Europe geared for "lean production"— a Japanese management style designed to lower production costs, raise efficiency, improve quality, and stimulate employee motivation. Lean production uses small groups of multi-skilled workers to perform particular tasks. Quality checks are immediate, and production can switch quickly from one model to another. Parts are delivered only as needed, reducing inventory costs.

CHAPTER 14

AUSTRALIA

- ECONOMIC STRUCTURE
- GROWTH IN THE EIGHTIES
- THE FOREIGN DEBT TRAP
- A TECHNOLOGICAL GAP
- AREAS OF TECHNICAL STRENGTH
- TECHNOLOGY POLICY
- ALLIANCE OPPORTUNITIES
- NEGOTIATING

Economic Structure

Australia is the world's smallest continent and the last to be discovered and settled by Europeans. Historically, the Australian economy was based on wool gathered from a huge sheep population, and raw materials extracted through mining. Even today, Australia accounts for half the world's production of fine wool, while metals and minerals account for more than a quarter of the country's exports.

Diagram 16   Map of Australia

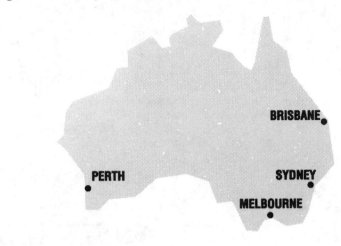

Australia's most important domestic industrial activities include wool production, the processing of iron, steel, or refined metals, and food production. Despite this strong resource-based orientation, the country is highly urbanized, with more than 80 percent of the population of 17.3 million living in towns and cities and half of it concentrated in Sydney and Melbourne.

Growth in the 1980s

The Australian economy started growing rapidly during the mid-1980s. Driven by a combination of low interest rates and strong consumer demand, real GDP grew by about 4 percent a year between 1985 and 1989. Australia's per capita GDP now stands at A$ 18,920. Strong growth was accompanied by high levels of inflation, however, exceeding 7 percent per annum by the end of the decade. To manage the inflationary pressures, now at 7.3 percent, the government has cut back spending and adopted policies designed to push interest rates higher.

The Foreign Debt Trap

Australia's rapid growth was supported by an explosion of imports. Companies and private consumers looked to foreign suppliers to supplement whatever was missing from the domestic economy, with the result that by mid-1989, net foreign debt exceeded $93.6 billion, with an account deficit of $16.1 billion. As foreign

Australian Business Payments and Receipts for Technical Know-how (in $ millions)

	1984/5	1986/7
Payments	172.9	257.5
Receipts	37.5	98.7

Source: *Year Book Australia.*

debt mounted, so too did servicing costs. In 1988-89 interest payments on the foreign debt reached $9.5 billion.

As it moves deeper into the 1990s, Australia faces significant economic challenges. The national debt continues to grow, labor costs are high, recessionary trends throughout the OECD have weakened the demand for Australian products, and high interest rates have undermined the position of several major Australian firms, forcing dramatic restructuring.

A Technological Gap

The most basic economic challenge facing Australia is to improve the country's technological infrastructure, move to higher value-added activities, and expand technology-based exports. Medium- and low-technology goods continue to account for an ever-increasing bulk of Australia's exports. By contrast, high-technology-based exports remained flat through the mid-1980s.

Another sign of the technology gap is the fact that Australian companies pay more to acquire foreign technology than they receive from the sale of their own know-how. At least here, however, there is a positive sign: receipts are growing faster than payments.

Areas of Technical Strength

- Despite the technology gap, Australia has developed world- class status in several areas of advanced technology. The following are some of the country's leading technology sectors:

- Medical Research: Several Australians have won Nobel prizes for medicine, and the country's scientists have done pioneering work in areas of transplant surgery, fertility research, deafness, and genetic engineering.

- Communications: Australia leads the world in the development of low-density, long-distance communications that offer smaller nations affordable access to satellite communications. These systems have been exported to the Pacific, Africa, and Asia.

- Space Technology: Australia has long operated its own satellites to support domestic telecommunications, and is developing launch facilities that are located close to the equator and thus require less power to lift rockets into geostationary orbit. The Australian radio telescope in New South Wales is one of the world's most advanced.

- Computing: Australia is the manufacturing base for IBM computers that are exported to the Pacific and Asia. It is a leader in data-management technology based on CD-ROMs. Australian software is used in robot tool control.

- Energy: Australia is a leader in solar power for water-heating systems, and has developed a system to produce household electricity from solar power.

- Automotive Industry: Five large companies produce 400,000 vehicles a year, some of which are exported to Japan and the United States. Automotive components are sent to Japan, Europe (especially Germany), and the U.S.

- Metal and Mineral Processing: Australia is a leader in the production of zirconia powders, rare earths, gallium, silicon, and advanced industrial materials, as well as the development of new smelting techniques and specialty steels.

- Transportation Equipment: Australia is known for the production of aircraft, passenger and vehicle ferries, trawlers, sailboats, and small naval craft.

Australia's Technology Policy

Since 1983, Australian government policy has aimed to accelerate the shift to higher-value-added manufacturing. The government has made agreements with trade unions to remove the restrictive practices that impede structural adjustment; it has offered financial assistance to businesses to invest in upgrading their operations; and it has removed tariff protection to force Australian companies to become more internationally competitive.

Major Trading Partners: Top Export Markets (1989)
(percent of total exports)

Japan	27.1
U.S.	10.3
South Korea	5.3
New Zealand	4.4
Canada	1.3

Total Exports (1989): $33.7 billion

Major Trading Partners: Top Import Suppliers (1989)
(percent of total imports)

U.S.	20.1
Japan	18.1
U.K.	6.0
West Germany	5.6
Canada	2.1

Total Exports (1989): $36.8 billion

To build the technology base, the Australian government is promoting expanded R&D activities. Just one of many national and state R&D incentive programs offers companies a 150 percent tax concession on R&D expenditures. The tax concessions were introduced in 1985, and will be available until 1993.

At the same time, government-sponsored research centers throughout the country bring together academic and industrial researchers to widen the country's scientific and industrial base. As a result of these efforts, gross expenditure on R&D has increased from $2.5 billion in 1984-85 to $3.3 billion in 1987-88.

Even so, Australian R&D remains a small percentage of its GNP. In 1987-88, the country spent only 1.2 percent of its GDP on R&D, while Japan spent 2.9 percent. As a result, Australia is attempting to get a better return on its R&D investment by encouraging collaborative research with partners abroad.

Given the structural similarities in the Canadian and Australian economies, and their common interests in extractive and advanced technologies, there are significant opportunities for technological cooperation between the two countries.

Technological Focus

In its efforts to enhance the technological base, Australia is building on its existing technological achievements and is paying special attention to the following sectors:

- *steel production, specialty steels*

- *motor vehicles and transport equipment*

- *fabricated metal products*

- *heavy engineering*

- *chemicals*

- *paper, printing and publishing*

- *textiles, clothing, and footwear*

- *biotechnology*

- *information systems*

- *waste management*

- *medical equipment*

- *advanced manufacturing*

- *aerospace*

Strategic Alliance Opportunities

Australia needs both foreign technology and market access if it is to improve its export performance. Because of this, the future should see a larger proportion of smaller Australian firms actively seeking partners abroad.

Some of these investors seek technology that will enable them to restructure Australia's mature industries such as mining and agriculture. Others need technology to develop new industries such as aerospace, biotechnology, and environmental protection. Encouraged by the Australian government's efforts to promote R&D cooperation and strategic alliances, technology-seeking companies are less interested in foreign acquisitions; they are more on the lookout for foreign partners.

The mining, automotive, and transportation sectors in Australia and North America could benefit from cooperative ventures designed to share technology and provide each other with market access. There are also opportunities to engage in joint R&D and technology transfers in aerospace, biotechnology, computer software, forestry, industrial machinery, waste management, chemical production, medical research, and environmental protection. Shared interests also exist in the fields of telecommunications and satellite technology.

Negotiating With Australians

North Americans will find it easier to negotiate with Australians than with most other nationalities in the Asia-Pacific region. Canada and Australia in particular have similarly structured economies, relatively small but highly concentrated populations, and rugged terrain that has demanded a focus on transportation and telecommunications. Both countries have similar colonial experiences, Commonwealth ties, British legal and political institutions, high standards of living, and a multicultural society that includes aboriginal peoples and individuals who originated from virtually every part of the globe.

CHAPTER 15

JAPAN

- ECONOMIC STRUCTURE
- EMPHASIS ON CONSENSUS
- HIGHER VALUE-ADDED
- ALLIANCE OPPORTUNITIES
- NEGOTIATING

Economic Structure

Japan boasts the second largest economy among developed nations. The two most striking characteristics of the Japanese economy are the speed with which Japan has achieved its position, and the extent to which its phenomenal growth has been based on trade.

In 1960, Japan's total trade (exports plus imports) amounted to $8.3 billion and accounted for 3.5 percent of world trade. By 1989, Japan's total trade had grown to $570.6 billion and its share of world trade had climbed to 8.2 percent.

Diagram 17 Map of Japan

Major Trading Partners: Top Export Markets (1989) (percent of total exports)

U.S.	34.2
South Korea	6.0
West Germany	5.8
Hong Kong	4.2
Canada	2.5

Total Exports (1989): $325.3 billion

Major Trading Partners: Top Import Suppliers (percent of total exports)

U.S.	23.0
South Korea	6.2
Australia	5.5
China	5.3
Canada	4.1

Total Exports (1989): $325.3 billion

Exports led this expansion. In 1960, Japan's imports and exports were roughly in balance. By 1989, Japan's exports totaled $323.2 billion and its imports were only $247.4 billion, a trade surplus of $75.8 billion.

An Emphasis on Consensus

This striking economic success has been based on a uniquely Japanese approach to domestic economic activity that seeks harmony and consensus. That approach has included:

- a general acceptance of close coordination between the activities of business and government;

- restrictions on destructive internal competition between Japanese companies and avoidance of hostile corporate takeovers;

- cooperation and information-sharing among firms, coupled with a reluctance to damage each other's commercial interests;

- strong ties of loyalty between companies in a supplier-client relationship;

- guarantees of lifetime employment in companies as a means of securing the loyalty of employees;

- formal and informal measures inhibiting foreign import penetration, and;

- a low-interest-rate policy and controls on the direction of bank lending.

Key elements of this traditional approach are changing, however. For example, the Japanese government has recently encouraged a more market-oriented approach to many economic practices by adopting policies promoting financial and trade liberalization. It is also government policy to reduce Japan's dependence on exports as the engine of growth, and to encourage domestic demand to attract imports and balance Japan's trade surplus.

The Shift to Higher Value-Added

The Japanese economy is also undergoing profound restructuring. Japan's original export drive was fueled by low-end manufactured goods that competed on price. The proceeds from that early success went into creating a heavy industrial base in sectors such as steel and shipbuilding.

The oil shocks of the 1970s and 1980s hit such heavy industries hard. As a resource-poor country dependent on foreign raw materials, Japan became conscious of its dependence on foreign supplies of energy and raw materials. Japanese industry tried to reduce that dependency by rationalizing existing industries and emphasizing energy efficiency. At the same time, Japan refocused its economic emphasis away from heavy industry and toward higher-value-added activities and advanced technologies.

This shift can be seen in the evolution of Japanese exports. In the 1960s and early 1970s, the heavy and chemical industries dominated exports, reaching as high as 82 percent of Japan's total exports.

Today, the list is topped by non-electrical and electrical machinery and equipment ($232.5 billion in 1989) and motor vehicles ($57.6 billion). Since 1983, the fastest growing industrial sectors have been consumer electronics, semiconductor integrated circuits, and passenger cars.

In the past, most of Japan's manufacturing know-how was imported from other countries through licensing agreements. For example, in 1969, payments made by Japan for foreign technology were eight times its technology receipts. What was once a heavy dependence on foreign technology is being transformed, however. By 1988, Japan's technology payments were a mere three times that of its technology receipts.

There are still those who argue that Japan's strong suit is to copy and adapt the technology invented by others. To prove them wrong, Japan is now focusing on doing its own basic research to reinforce its product and process technology, and reduce its dependence on foreign solutions.

Basic research now accounts for 13.3 percent of all the R&D performed in Japan, and these efforts are being concentrated in fields such as biotechnology, medicine, satellites, telecommunications, computer software, and the environment. More than 80 percent of R&D is done by private research establishments, though the government sets an overall direction through incentives and national programs in strategic areas.

The Boom in Japanese Foreign Direct Investment

	Amount ($ billions)	Growth Over Previous Year (%)
1985	16.7	—
1986	30.9	85.0
1987	44.3	43.4
1988	57.8	30.5
1989	79.6	37.7

Source: Japanese Ministry of Finance. (notification basis)

The Japanese recognize, however, that they cannot do everything themselves. Japan's White Paper on Science and Technology (1989) stresses the need for technological cooperation and scientific exchanges with other countries. Japan is in a strong position. Today, it holds 50 percent of the world's patents, putting it in a powerful bargaining position as it seeks technology partners abroad.

The White Paper also recommends developing offshore R&D facilities that can enhance the access of Japanese firms to technology around the globe. A desire to acquire technology has become an important factor driving Japanese investment overseas.

Strategic Alliance Opportunities

Japan's huge trade surpluses have given its exporting companies both the means and a variety of motivations to invest in overseas markets:

- Because Japan is poor in natural resources, some overseas investments are focused on securing access to raw materials.

- As a result of its own industrial restructuring, Japan is actively seeking foreign technologies or technological partnerships, especially in priority areas such as biotechnology, medicines, satellites, telecommunications, computer software, and advanced industrial materials.

- There is considerable foreign unease over Japan's huge trade surpluses: FDI (foreign direct investment) is a way of circumventing emerging trade barriers.

- An increasing number of Japanese firms are becoming sensitive to the desire of their foreign partners to develop their own production and value-added activities in Japan.

- Japan is experiencing a shortage of skilled labor at home and seeks to access foreign pools of labor.

- Many large Japanese firms see opportunities for reducing costs by investing in plants located in low-cost countries.

- Appreciation of the yen has made overseas investments seem relatively inexpensive for Japanese investors.

- An increasing number of Japanese firms are aware of the need to globalize their economic activities in order to take advantage of global procurement networks and international divisions of labor.

Despite developed international linkages, many Japanese companies have been slow to manufacture abroad. In 1988, the overseas production ratio of Japanese manufacturers was only 4.8 percent, compared to a U.S. ratio of 21 percent and a West German ratio of 17 percent. Overseas production is, however, expected to rise to about 8 percent of total manufacturing by 1995. The current boom in Japanese FDI is focused on plants that supply both local and Japanese markets.

Japanese companies are moving into comprehensive strategic alliances that transfer design and development abroad, in addition to production. The Japanese seem increasingly willing to share some of their know-how with local managers and some of their R&D with foreign partners. This will free Japanese designers back home to concentrate their efforts on more advanced technologies.

Coupled to this, Japanese companies are beginning to decentralize head-office functions, internationalize their management, and increase overseas procurement of components (sometimes by offering to transfer technology).

Japanese-U.S. Alliances in the Steel Industry

The world steel industry is forging new international links, and much of this activity has taken the form of joint ventures between U.S. and Japanese firms. The U.S. steel firms want access to Japanese technology. The Japanese invest 1.5 percent of sales in research and development, compared to 0.5 percent in the U.S. An example of Japanese leadership is their cold-rolling plants, which can finish a metal coil in one hour rather than the traditional 12 days. The Japanese have established a considerable stake in the U.S. industry and they want better access to the U.S. market, particularly as suppliers to the growing number of Japanese car manufacturers in the U.S.

U.S.-Japanese Joint Ventures

Nucor - Yamato Kogyo (beams)
Armco - Kawasaki (steel finishing)
Inland - Nippon (cold rolling and galvanizing)
Wheeling Pittsburgh - Nisshin (coated sheet)
LTV - Sumito (steel finishing)

The desire to access new technologies has led many Japanese firms into strategic alliances. This is especially true among car manufacturers, parts makers, and semiconductor manufacturers. Strategic alliances are very popular among SMEs, which value their partners' knowledge of local conditions.

Today, Japanese investors offer more than financing: they offer expertise. Japanese investors bring with them proven international competitive abilities, management skills, and excellent engineering and technological capabilities, as well as the financial resources to make things happen.

The Japanese have an open policy toward outbound investment, because it is an effective way to reduce their trade surplus. The foreign exchange and foreign

Japanese Investment Abroad, Cumulative Totals (1951-1989) (in $ billions)

United States	163.7
United Kingdom	17.2
Panama	16.2
Australia	13.5
Indonesia	11.3
Netherlands	11.0
Hong Kong	8.8
Cayman Islands	7.3
Brazil	6.4
Singapore	6.7
Luxembourg	5.9
Canada	5.0

Source: Japan External Trade Organization.

trade control law of 1980 freed outbound and inbound investment, while the Plaza Agreement of 1985 encourages globalization by allowing the yen to appreciate. Moreover, Japan's domestic infrastructure, unlike South Korea's and Taiwan's, supports companies interested in venturing overseas. Japanese financial institutions, for example, have become effective go-betweens in corporate transactions.

A Business Triangle

Komag, Inc. of California and two Japanese companies, Kobe Steel Ltd. and Asahi Glass Co. Ltd., have developed a number of joint ventures and strategic alliances. Komag manufactures and markets data-storage discs. The California company wanted to exert more control over its supply of aluminum substrate, a product used as the basis of the recording material in the discs Komag builds. Kobe Steel was Komag's primary supplier of the raw aluminum used to form the aluminum substrate. Together, they formed a joint venture called Komag Materials Technology.

With a majority share, Komag, Inc. manages and operates the venture. Kobe has a $1.5 million share, supplies raw aluminum, and will have access to any new technology the joint venture develops. Komag is the only customer.

The venture will supply as much as 80 percent of Komag's substrate needs, with Kobe supplying the rest.

In order to staff and locate the joint venture, Komag Inc. acquired an entire company, DMT of California. The venture is using all of DMT's 150 employees, as well as hiring new employees.

In 1987, Komag formed a Japanese joint venture with two Japanese firms, Asahi Glass Co. Ltd. and Vacuum Metallurgical Co. The venture manufactures and sells computer discs. Komag owns 50 percent of the venture, while Asahi owns most of the remainder. Kobe Steel is the major supplier of aluminum substrates to this venture as well.

In the meantime, Kobe Steel and Asahi are working together to develop substrates made from glass, freeing the two companies from their dependency on aluminum.

Negotiating With the Japanese

In entering into business dealings with the Japanese, pay attention to cultural issues and differences in negotiating style. The Japanese do not expect foreigners to understand the details of their own etiquette, but you should make an effort to conform to the most important Japanese customs.

Japanese names appear with the family name last. Always use the family name preceded by Mr., Mrs., or Miss. If you establish good rapport, you may use the suffix "san" after the family name, which is equivalent to "Mister."

The Japanese are very punctual. Make your appointments as far in advance as possible and then be on time, or even a few minutes early. If you have an appointment with a senior executive, a junior staff member will probably entertain you in a lounge with tea or coffee prior to the meeting.

When your key contact arrives, rise to be introduced and exchange business cards. Business cards are very important in Japan and they are examined carefully. Yours should have your name, the name of your company, and your title or position within the company. Your card should carry a Japanese translation on one side, and this can be prepared fairly quickly by a local printer. The card should be well-printed, using the same quality on both sides, and it should not carry advertising slogans.

Do not expect much from your first meeting: its basic purpose is to establish an atmosphere of friendliness and harmony. Compliments are exchanged, but never jokes, and sincerity is crucial. Impersonal gifts are frequently given, and these should be elegant and of the very best quality. Subsequent meetings will focus on building a good relationship, since the Japanese are interested in stable, long-term associations with compatible partners.

The Japanese often conduct formal negotiations through several teams. Each team may go over the same issues to ensure that they understand every aspect of your proposal. Be patient, sincere, and forthcoming. Be prepared for long negotiations before the Japanese come to a decision, but once a decision is made, be ready for instantaneous implementation.

The spokesman for the Japanese side may be the person that speaks English the best rather than the leader of the negotiations. To ensure that you understand all the details and that you are properly understood, you should employ your own translators.

Japanese culture places a high premium on consensus and harmony. Conversely, the Japanese strive to avoid unpleasantness and confrontation. As a result, businesses rarely take each other to court. They will be offended if you take a lawyer to your meetings or present them with a draft contract prematurely.

The Japanese also do not like complicated legal documents. Contracts cover the essential points but leave both parties leeway to make adjustments as the need arises. The Japanese expect both parties to be able to alter implementation as circumstances change. Remember that Japanese businessmen do not feel bound by any verbal discussions, or by any document until they have affixed their personal seal to it.

Patience, Trust, and Loyalty Key to Japanese Partnerships

It took Gennum, a Canadian electronics company specializing in miniature audio amplifiers for hearing aids, 15 years to develop its Japanese business, partly because the company had to learn that marketing in Japan works differently than in North America. "In North American and Europe, we're used to making a pitch for our product and technology, and then letting it stand by itself," says Gennum CEO Douglas Barber. "But nothing stands by itself in Japan, where the human dimension is a bigger factor in business."

Gennum found the keys to marketing in Japan were not carefully worded legal documents, but patience, trust, and loyalty. Gennum initially worked its way into the complex web of business connections required for successful Japanese marketing by partnering with Sanshin Enterprise Co., a small Tokyo-based trading house. Gennum sold its products to Sanshin, which in turn resold them to its customers. Sanshin facilitated introductions and meetings between Gennum staff and Japanese buyers, and helped its partner overcome the language barrier. As Gennum gained confidence in its ability to function on its own, it wanted more direct, ongoing contact with its customers. In 1989 it opened its own Tokyo sales office, which by 1992 accounted for approximately two-thirds of Japanese sales. (Report on Business, Globe and Mail, *April 1992, pp. 39, 40)*

On rare occasions you may be invited to a private home in Japan. If this occurs, you should reciprocate with an invitation to dinner in a private room of a restaurant. Remember that shoes are removed before entering Japanese-style houses and restaurants. When sitting on the floor, men can cross their legs and take jackets off after the initial toast. At large formal dinners it is common to sing songs, and you should have one ready, just in case.

CHAPTER 16

SOUTH KOREA

- **ECONOMIC STRUCTURE**
- **TRANSFORMATION**
- **WARNING SIGNS**
- **TECHNOLOGY DEPENDENCY**
- **ALLIANCE OPPORTUNITIES**
- **NEGOTIATING**

Economic Structure

The Republic of Korea has one of the most consistent and remarkable growth records of any economy in the world. Since 1970, the country's economy has grown at an average of more than 8 percent each year. Between 1986 and 1988 annual growth rates averaged more than 12 percent.

Manufacturing has been, and continues to be, the base of the Korean economy, accounting for 31.6 percent of GDP in 1989. Key industries include steel, electronics, automobiles, shipbuilding, and heavy machinery

Electronics is the fastest-growing of the industrial sectors. In 1988, Korea exported $4.7 billion worth of electronic components—nearly three times the $1.8

Diagram 18   Map of South Korea

Major Trading Partners: Top Export Markets (1989) (percent of total exports)

U.S.	33.4
Japan	21.8
Hong Kong	5.5
West Germany	3.4
Canada	3.1

Total Exports (1989): $73.9 billion

Major Trading Partners: Top Import Suppliers (1989) (percent of total imports)

Japan	28.5
U.S.	25.7
West Germany	4.2
Australia	3.7
Canada	2.7

Total Imports (1989): $72.8 billion

billion exported in 1984. Korea has been especially successful with semiconductors. In 1989, it produced $5.7 billion worth of computer chips, rivaling the United States and Japan as a producer of integrated circuits.

An Ongoing Transformation

Today's South Korean economy is the product of a systematic and ongoing transformation that reaches back four decades to the end of the Korean War.

In the late 1950s and through the 1960s, the Koreans focused on import substitution. They then expanded their export-oriented light manufacturing industries, such as clothing and textiles, and encouraged the development of producer-goods industries. By the 1970s, the Korean economy was expanding into heavy and chemical industries, and shifting its emphasis from the importing of foreign capital to the acquisition of foreign technology. At the same time, the competitiveness of the country's export-oriented industries was strengthened.

In the 1980s, the Koreans began to focus on technology-intensive sectors, encouraging the development of highly skilled labor and improving productivity. During this period, their earlier reliance on clothing and textiles ended, while steel and electronics came into prominence. This process of technological upgrading will continue through the 1990s as the Koreans adjust their industrial structure to meet changing world conditions, seek to improve productivity, and promote balanced regional development within the country.

To date, large companies known as *chaebols* have been the backbone of Korean development. Even so, the government has played a major role in the country's economic policy, writing detailed plans for each industrial sector. Recently, the government has begun to focus on encouraging small and medium-sized enterprises by providing venture capital, low-cost loans and R&D incentives.

Warning Signs

There have been signs, of late, that Korea's export-oriented formula for success may have to undergo some revision.

Exports grew by only 10 percent in 1989, resulting in a narrowing of the country's account surplus and less liquidity in the economy. This, in turn, means that overall economic growth slowed in 1989, though it was a still impressive 7 percent. There were other warning signs, however.

Korea's rapid expansion has absorbed most of the available work force. As a result, unemployment remains enviably low. In 1988, for example, it was only 2.5 percent of the work force, and demand for labor remains strong.

Korean workers, however, have begun to demand a greater share of the benefits that economic success brings. Strikes and labor unrest are pushing wages up. As a result, the country is losing its original advantage as a low-wage producer.

At the same time, export success has led to inflationary pressures at home. Inflation ran at 7.1 percent in 1988 and 6 percent in 1989, fueled in part by real estate speculation, which drove up land costs in a country that is among the most densely populated in Asia.

These changes mean that Korean products have lost some of their cost advantages in the international marketplace. In response, some Korean companies are focusing on domestic markets where economic and social transformation has led to strong and growing demand. The other response is to emphasize technological skills and move into higher-value-added exports.

Technology Dependency

Any attempt by Korea to move into high-value-added export activities is complicated by the fact that the country is dependent on foreign technology. For example, in 1989, Korea exported $12.4 million of its own technology, while importing $1 billion in foreign technology.

Korea's technological dependency stems from a tendency of its companies to import technology rather than do their own R&D. The traditional pattern has been for Korean companies to license other people's technology, and then improve the manufacturing processes associated with that technology.

The Korean government is determined to reduce the country's technological dependence by supporting the acquisition of core technologies that will allow the country to perform more of its own R&D activity. The government hopes its Seven-Year Plan for High-Technology and Industry Development will make Korea one of the world's leading technological powers by the year 2000.

Korean R&D expenditure has grown from $692 million (0.9 percent of GDP) in 1981 to $6.25 billion (2.6 percent of GDP) in 1989. Under the government's technology plan, R&D expenditure is expected to expand by 15 percent each year until 1995. The objective is for R&D activities to reach 3 percent of GDP by the year 2001. The overall objective for the 1990s is to expand the resources available for scientific and technical activity, and to promote industrial efficiency.

Korea's R&D efforts are broadly based. The country is developing advanced technologies for industrial and commercial application, basic scientific research, and technologies associated with social welfare.

The private sector has been assigned applied research projects for commercialization. The universities are doing basic research, and the government is pursuing R&D in key industrial technologies that are of public interest, especially in energy and resources, health, and the environment.

The Republic of South Korea's Ministry of Trade and Industry is emphasizing seven strategic industrial sectors in its bid to encourage the development of applied and commercial technologies:

- microelectronics

- factory automation

- new materials

- fine chemicals

- biotechnology

- optics

- aerospace

Government goals in these areas will facilitate the development of appropriate infrastructure as well as promoting increased R&D activity.

Complementing this industrial focus will be an emphasis on basic research performed largely by the universities. This activity will focus on:

- information industries

- semiconductors

- automation

- new materials

- biotechnology

- fine chemicals

- new energy technology

- aerospace

- transportation

- medicine

- the environment

- lasers

- superconductivity

- hydrogen power

- sensors

- catalysts

The private sector is being offered a number of incentives to play its assigned part in Korea's technology drive. For example, the government is encouraging

SMEs to enter into R&D consortia at a suggested ratio of 50 companies for every R&D center. At the same time, Korea is also looking to increase its participation in multinational joint technology development projects.

During the early phases of Korea's industrial evolution, the government imposed tight controls on outward direct investment in order to keep capital at home for domestic development. The small amount of FDI permitted was channeled into resource-based ventures designed to supply Korean industry with raw materials. With strong export growth, Korea began to accumulate significant reserves of capital, which exceeded the absorptive capacity of the domestic economy. To minimize the inflationary impact of these reserves, Korea allowed companies to invest them abroad. As a result, Korean investments overseas have increased rapidly in recent years.

In 1988, the Korean government opened an office within the Export-Import Bank of Korea to provide companies with information on foreign investment. It also raised the limit on official approval for investments from $246,000 to $615,000. In 1989, this threshold was raised to $2.4 million, and the government lifted earlier restrictions limiting investment to natural resource companies. This liberal atmosphere changed somewhat when an increase in foreign direct investment coincided with a shrinkage in current account surplus.

In July of 1990, the Ministry of Finance introduced tighter investment screening procedures, requiring a certificate of validity for investments greater than $35 million; for joint ventures valued at more than $56 million in which the Korean side owns more than 50 percent of the venture; and for investments larger than $6 million that exceed the net capital of the Korean business making them.

The limit on loans by the Export-Import Bank of Korea has also been lowered from 80-90 percent of the investment to 60-80 percent.

Strategic Alliance Opportunities

Because the Koreans have developed an expertise in commercializing and exploiting foreign technology, they tend to look for strategic alliances that give them access to technology while allowing them to contribute their own manufacturing expertise. At the same time, Korean firms are investing heavily in developing their own technology, and the companies who partner with them stand to reap rich rewards.

Korean companies are interested in avoiding trade barriers, expanding market access, acquiring new technologies, and securing natural resources. Koreans view offshore production plants as a means of circumventing trade restrictions imposed by other countries. In the past, these restrictions have hampered Korea's ability to establish its own brand names.

Koreans believe they must establish themselves in key markets around the world if they are to be effective competitors in the future. They particularly want to expand into the North American market, and find the Canada-U.S. Free Trade

Agreement attractive in that it allows them to combine access to Canadian resources with access to the U.S. market.

Rising labor costs and labor unrest in Korea have led many of its labor-intensive industries to relocate to other countries in Southeast Asia. Nevertheless, by 1990, approximately 40 percent of Korea's total stock of foreign direct investment was in North America, concentrated in manufacturing (37 percent), mining (28 percent) and trading activities (13 percent).

Korea is interested in acquiring technology through licenses and alliances. Opportunities for strategic alliances exist in communications, transportation, natural resources, bioengineering, mechatronics (numerically controlled machine tools), industrial robots, CAD/CAM, programmable logic controllers, sensors, and servomotors.

In the aerospace industry, Korea is looking for design techniques and new lightweight, hard materials. There is also a strong demand for aircraft components, maintenance equipment, avionics, and engines.

There are approximately 500 Korean companies that manufacture environmental-control equipment, but most are SMᵣ₃ unable to engineer highly sophisticated instruments and control equipment. Firms in this sector that are registered with the Korean government can negotiate technology transfers and joint ventures with foreign companies.

The Korean Telecommunications Authority is completing a five-year program to invest $9.4 billion in capital expenditures designed to increase communications technology in Korea. One goal has been to increase the number of phones from 18 to 22 per 100 persons. Samsung, Daewoo, and Goldstar have joint ventures with AT&T, Ericsson, and Siemens. In addition, the National Priority Plan has targeted telecommunications switching products and private branch exchanges (PBXs) for large-scale manufacturing and distribution worldwide. North American companies can try to link up with the marketing arm of the *chaebols* and exchange technology in these areas for access to world markets.

Negotiating With Koreans

Koreans are sensitive to the intangible factors that influence personal conduct and relationships among people. They call this *kibun*, and they say that if it is good, one functions smoothly. In their negotiations, Koreans try to enhance the *kibun* of both sides because they feel that to damage it will terminate a relationship, or even create an enemy.

Protocol and proper acknowledgement of each other's position are extremely important to Koreans. It is therefore advisable to have a formal introduction to your Korean counterpart, and the use of an intermediary may be advisable, because if your prospect respects the intermediary, he will probably also respect you. Indeed, Koreans tend to treat the representative of a person or group with more care than the group itself, because the substitute may be more sensitive to slights.

Korean society is hierarchical, and no business person is comfortable with another until his company and position are known. Business cards are very important in establishing one's place in the social order, but cards are also essential because Koreans tend not to use personal names. They believe that one's name is personal property, and that personal names should be honored and respected. Actually pronouncing a name can be seen as presumptuous and impolite, and Koreans prefer to greet each other by a title (e.g., Director) or some other honorific designation.

In business, flattery is a way of life. It is considered indelicate to start immediately or abruptly on the main points of a transaction. Discussions start with peripheral matters and only gradually move to the center. It will enhance personal rapport if you display some knowledge of the remarkable changes Korean society has undergone, and express admiration for Korea's successes and achievements.

The Koreans are careful not to give offense and seek to establish harmonious personal relations. That is why it is important to personalize your dealings with your Korean partners. Find out as much as possible about their status, hobbies, philosophy, and even their birthdays.

During negotiations, be patient, gentle, firm, and dignified. Formal behavior is required at all times, and this even extends to the posture adopted during discussions. Do not push too hard and, if possible, leave sensitive issues and details for go-betweens so as not to impair your own relationship with the company president or CEO.

Do not assume your Korean counterpart understands everything you say, even if he is extending you the courtesy of speaking English. His English may not be as good as you think, and there are also cultural differences that may impair understanding.

Western logic does not always have an impact on Koreans, who may be more persuaded by personal factors. And remember that when the Koreans say "yes," they may only mean "I heard you," and may not be agreeing with what you have said.

For Koreans, human relationships and informal understandings with trusted partners are more important than formal contracts. Contracts are seen to be significant because of who signed them and the fact of their existence, but they should also be flexible enough to fit changing circumstances. And give Koreans time to come to a decision.

When dealing with Koreans, the giving of small gifts is accepted and recommended. They also like to entertain, and you should participate and reciprocate if invited to do so. Going out for drinks with your hosts or attending parties are two common forms of entertainment. Recently, taking part in a golf game has become increasingly popular within the business community.

CHAPTER 17

SINGAPORE

- **ECONOMIC STRUCTURE**
- **OPEN TRADING**
- **ECONOMIC DEVELOPMENT BOARD**
- **ALLIANCE OPPORTUNITIES**
- **SECTORS OF OPPORTUNITY**
- **NEGOTIATING**

Economic Structure

Singapore is an independent city-state covering about 242 square miles (626 square kilometers) of territory and consisting of the island of Singapore and 54 adjacent islands. Approximately 77 percent of its population is of Chinese descent, with the remainder largely made up of Malays and Indians. With no natural resources, Singapore has based its prosperity on an industrious, educated, and productive labor force and a strategic geographic location.

Economic success, coupled with concerted efforts by the government, has given Singapore an excellent infrastructure. Its port is the busiest in world, handling 34,000 ships in 1988.

Diagram 19 Map of Singapore

A pioneer in the use of paperless customs procedures, Singapore attracts businesses interested in quick turnaround of their shipping. The Singapore airport is one of world's best, and certainly the best in Southeast Asia. Recently expanded and upgraded, it now has an annual capacity of 20 million passengers.

Singapore also enjoys sophisticated telecommunications facilities and a developed financial infrastructure and it is recognized as an international business center for commercial services, engineering support, and medical care.

After achieving independence in 1965, Singapore embarked on a policy of rapid industrialization. The strategy of import substitution had limited application, however, because of the city's small domestic market. Instead, it concentrated on manufacturing for export. The government also focused on developing the entrepôt activities of trading, processing, storing, banking, insurance, repackaging, marketing, transportation, and communications.

As a result, Singapore has one of the fastest-growing economies in the world. Growth has been especially strong after 1985, ranging from 7 to 10 percent a year. This expansion has been accompanied by relative price stability and one of the highest savings rates in the world. The only significant economic problem is a labor shortage—the inevitable result of rapid growth.

By 1990 manufacturing constituted about 26 percent of Singapore's GDP, and employed about 45 percent of its work force. The major focus is on electrical and electronics products, petroleum products, chemicals, food and beverages, fabricated metal products, transport equipment, textiles, and garments. Interestingly, the average wage in Singapore's manufacturing sector is higher than in any other developing country, but it is the lowest for all occupational groups in Singapore, even lower than for agriculture and fishing.

The Most Open Trading Nation in the World

Singapore's economic success has been based on importing components or materials, assembling or processing them, and then exporting them to foreign markets. Approximately 35 percent of the goods exported from Singapore are re-exports, and most of the goods imported into the city are similarly destined for re-export. In 1990, Singapore's total trade (exports plus imports) amounted to $99.3 billion, more than three times its GDP of $31.73 billion.

Because Singapore is one of the world's most trade-oriented countries, it is also highly sensitive to changes in the international economic environment. With the softening of the U.S. economy in 1990, Singapore's decreasing exports to the U.S. have been replaced by Asian market exports.

Singapore's corporations are now attempting to diversify their export markets by seeking trade opportunities in Japan and Western Europe. Meanwhile, Singapore's exports to Canada have moved from resource-based goods to electronics and manufacturing.

Singapore's economy is marked by complete economic freedom of ownership, capital movements, and trade. In order to promote growth, the government actively sought investment from the world's developed economies. Foreign investors were encouraged to establish in Singapore, using the country as a platform from which to do business within the entire region. By 1990 there were about 5,000 foreign companies active in Singapore, accounting for approximately 70 percent of the country's domestic exports.

Initially, the government of Singapore was also active in every sector of the economy. By 1990, it still owned about 450 companies in key industries such as shipbuilding and petrochemicals, employing about 58,000 out of a labor force of just over a million. The government is presently moving toward greater privatization.

The remainder of the economy consists of 70,000 mostly small and medium-sized businesses. As late as 1990, Singapore had no indigenous multinationals or general trading companies, although the government continues to encourage Singaporean firms to expand abroad.

Initially, Singapore concentrated on labor-intensive manufacturing in sectors such as textiles. By the late 1980s, however, computer components and other electronics had become the most important focus for manufacturing.

Singapore's ability to develop technology-intensive industries is being promoted by the government, which has assumed a significant role in R&D activities. At the same time, many international technology-based firms are locating in Singapore to assemble electronic products and to perform R&D.

Economic Development Board

Singapore's Economic Development Board is a semi-autonomous body that plans and implements industrial policy. Acting as the main instrument of the

**Major Trading Partners: Top Export Markets (1989)
(percent of total exports)**

U.S.	23.3
Malaysia	13.7
Japan	8.5
Hong Kong	6.3
Canada	0.9

Total Exports (1989): $53.2 billion

**Major Trading Partners: Top Import Suppliers (1989)
(percent of total imports)**

Japan	21.3
U.S.	17.1
Malaysia	13.2
Other Asia NES	4.9
Canada	0.5

Total Imports (1989): $58.9 billion

government's industrial policy, it provides incentives to investors and assists them in obtaining land, factory space, financing, and skilled manpower. It has been used to promote and develop the manufacturing sectors, and recently has focused its attention on a wide variety of skill- and knowledge-intensive areas, such as:

- biotechnology
- automation in manufacturing
- avionics and aero-engine components
- medical services, health care, and pharmaceutical industries
- leisure and exhibition services

- agrotechnology

- information technologies and integrated circuit design

- electronic systems in automobiles

- advanced plastics fabrication

- petrochemical products and specialty chemicals

- training of R&D personnel

- training in tool and die making

There is also a significant emphasis on high-value-added services such as finance, banking, transportation, and telecommunications.

Strategic Alliance Opportunities

Singaporeans have started to engage in significant strategic alliance initiatives. With an eye toward acquiring technology and securing access to new markets, the Economic Development Board has formed a strategic business unit to promote overseas investment. In 1988 the board launched the International Direct Investment program to encourage local companies to expand abroad through direct investments and strategic alliances, and eventually to develop into multinational corporations. To be eligible for its assistance, a company must be 50 percent Singaporean and take an active part in the management of an overseas company. Incentives include grants for feasibility studies, technical training, tax breaks for capital losses incurred overseas, and tax exemptions on repatriated profits.

The International Direct Investment Program complements a $120 million venture capital fund established in 1985. The fund is used for co-investing with local business people in new technology-intensive companies in Singapore and overseas; for investing in professional venture capital funds to gain windows on foreign technology; and for stimulating the emergence of a venture capital industry in Singapore.

Today, foreign investment is increasingly seen as a way to access or acquire technology, to expand and diversify markets, and to create Singaporean multinationals. Investments abroad, however, are expected to have some link to Singapore and its needs.

The key to attracting alliance partners from Singapore is to build a two-way relationship. Offering something of value to Singaporean companies in return for investment can involve technology, distribution and marketing rights, procurement, or manufacturing opportunities.

If North American companies are not prepared to offer technology, or if they are uninterested in establishing operations in Singapore, it is unlikely that the Singaporeans will be interested in expanding cooperation to the stage where alliances are possible.

Sectors of Opportunity

The most promising sectors for strategic alliance opportunities are those industries favored by Singapore's Economic Development Board.

Singapore's airport is the busiest in the region. It is used by all of the world's major airlines and is a recognized regional aircraft service center. As a result, there is a strong interest in aerospace industries, aircraft engine components, avionics, simulators, aircraft maintenance, and overhaul services. There are opportunities to cooperate with air carriers to provide equipment and services in Singapore, as well as to develop new aviation and aerospace technologies.

There are numerous opportunities in advanced technology products and services to complement Singapore's own growth objectives in this area. Information systems, advanced manufacturing, and electronics are areas of particular interest.

Negotiating in Singapore

It is relatively easy to do business with large Singaporean firms since many of them are subsidiaries of Western firms, and as such use Western systems of management. The smaller firms, however, are managed with loose organizational structures coupled to highly centralized decision-making. Because Singapore is characterized by a fast pace of life, business can be conducted quickly.

Despite its Chinese majority, Singapore reflects a cultural diversity. Many Asian cultural practices persist, but the Western handshake has become a common form of greeting, with the bow reserved for Asians. Courtesy demands that a person be addressed by the family name preceded by Mr., Mrs. or Miss. First names should not be used unless one is invited to do so.

Singaporeans are very punctual and expect punctuality from others. Unlike other Asians, they get down to business right away and do not spend time on pleasantries. They do not indulge in unnecessary or superficial smiling or familiarity, and restrict expressions of courtesy to people whom they know—others they treat with a formal neutrality.

Touching another person, especially on the head, is considered impolite. When crossing legs, place one knee directly over the other and do not point your foot or the sole of your foot at anyone. Avoid tapping or shaking your foot under the table while discussing business.

During the conduct of business, dinner invitations are frequent, and it is not uncommon to take guests out to restaurants virtually every night of the week.

CHAPTER 18

TAIWAN

- **ECONOMIC STRUCTURE**
- **INDUSTRIAL STRUCTURE**
- **FOCUS ON TECHNOLOGY**
- **ALLIANCE OPPORTUNITIES**
- **NEGOTIATING**

Economic Structure

Taiwan is a large island off the coast of mainland China. When the mainland was taken over by the Communists in 1949, the Nationalist government of Chiang Kai-shek retreated to Taiwan, where it has survived under the leadership of the Kuomintang party.

The People's Republic of China and the authorities on Taiwan each claim to be the sole legitimate government of China. This has forced the world to choose between recognizing the Republic of China on Taiwan or the People's Republic of China in Beijing. Most nations now recognize the government in Beijing, with the result that Taiwan has become something of an anomaly: a major economic powerhouse with virtually no diplomatic recognition by the world community.

Diagram 20   Map of Taiwan

The island of Taiwan is heavily populated, with over 20.5 million inhabitants, and it is poor in natural resources. As a result, the government looked to foreign trade to serve as the engine of growth, and it adopted a strategy of importing raw materials, processing them domestically, and exporting the finished products.

In the 1950s, Taiwan developed labor-intensive, import-substituting industries. When these succeeded in the 1960s, the government improved the domestic investment climate and established low-cost and low-value-added, export-oriented industries.

By the 1970s, Taiwan was developing basic and heavy industries. With this infrastructure in place, it adopted a more strategic orientation in the 1980s, emphasizing and promoting certain key industrial sectors, especially technology-based activities. As a result of this strategy, between 1953 and the end of 1989, Taiwan's economy grew at an average annual rate of 8.8 percent. Growth dipped to 5.0 percent in 1990 and rose again to 7.2 percent in 1991.

Taiwan's expansion culminated in 1987, when exports grew by 19 percent and GDP increased by 12.5 percent. Since then the economy has been cooling off. In 1991, exports grew by only 13 percent, while the GDP grew 7.2 percent.

To some extent, the slowdown was the inevitable result of earlier success. Strong export performance led to a domestic cash glut and the appreciation of the New Taiwan dollar, which made Taiwanese exports less competitive. At the same time, the export-led boom was being constrained by labor shortages, rising wages, increases in the costs of land, and new concerns about environmental degradation.

As a result, Taiwan has been experiencing significant inflationary pressures. In 1989, it was estimated that inflation was running at an annual rate of about 4.4

percent, but this was understated since the official basket of goods and services used to measure it was out of date, and no longer reflected the real spending patterns of the Taiwanese. In 1991, the official inflation rate dropped to 3.6 percent.

Rising domestic costs made Taiwanese exports less attractive at a time when Taiwan's trade partners were heading into recessions. As overseas demand fell, Taiwan's trade surplus shrank, as did its current account balance, and domestic investment in new plants weakened. By 1991, Taiwan's GDP grew by only 7.2 percent, still an impressive rate by Western standards, but low in terms of Taiwan's previous performance.

Traditionally, the government of Taiwan has been very involved in the economy, particularly in the energy, heavy industry, and financial sectors. Planning

Major Trading Partners: Top Export Markets (1989) (percent of total exports)

U.S.	23.3
Japan	13.7
Hong Kong	8.5
West Germany	6.3
Canada	0.9

Total Exports (1989): $78.4 billion

Major Trading Partners: Top Import Markets (1989) (percent of total imports)

U.S.	23.3
Malaysia	13.7
Japan	8.5
Hong Kong	6.3
Canada	0.9

	1989	1990	1991
Total Imports (in billions)	$61.9	$51.9	$60.7

usually took the form of suggestions from the government, backed up with sympathetic fiscal, monetary, and trade policies, and the provision of infrastructure.

In the mid 1980s, Taiwan began liberalizing its domestic regulatory regime and opening up its economy to foreign investors. As a result, there have been dramatic increases in foreign direct investment in Taiwan. FDI doubled in 1987, and doubled again in 1989 to $2.6 billion, totalling about $11.8 billion at the end of that year.

The Taiwanese government has become less involved in the economy, and public corporations are being privatized. The government realizes that financial restructuring is necessary to channel resources away from the stock market and into more productive areas.

The government continues to encourage businesses to invest in industries it sees as strategic, however. In the export market, the government is emphasizing consumer electronics, information systems, telecommunications, and automated production systems. In the domestic market, it is encouraging food processing, pharmaceuticals, biotechnology, and diagnostic imaging.

Industrial Structure

Small and medium-sized enterprises are the backbone of the Taiwanese economy, accounting for more than 80 percent of industrial production. Yet these companies tend to be undercapitalized: more than 90 percent have paid-up capital of less than $436,000. Few of them have a long-term international strategy to upgrade their operations and move into high-value-added activities.

Taiwan's initial strength was in labor-intensive manufacturing—particularly food processing, clothing and textiles, and "copy-cat" manufacturing using other people's technology. Although such industries have responded to rising wage costs better than those in many other countries, their first instinct is often to move existing operations to countries with low labor costs rather than to develop higher-value-added activities at home.

As a result, it is estimated that in 1988 and 1989 Taiwanese companies invested about $5.3 billion to establish new production facilities in lower-cost regions of Southeast Asia.

A New Technology Focus

The Taiwanese government is promoting restructuring of the economy in order to move more forcefully into technology-intensive and service industries. Some Taiwanese manufacturers have begun to focus on more sophisticated technologies, particularly computer components and parts, television sets, and calculators.

Yet many are finding it difficult to move to more modern management systems or to find qualified personnel to enhance their R&D activities. The smaller enterprises that dominate Taiwan's economy seldom have the resources needed to undertake major R&D projects. On average, Taiwan's companies spend 0.5 percent of sales on R&D—less than half of the average expenditure in South Korea.

The Taiwanese government plans to invest $17 billion in the development of advanced technologies by 1996. It is emphasizing the development of applied technologies and computer-driven R&D by funding specific high-tech projects, as well as the creation of new laboratories.

In addition, the Hsinchu Science Park was established in 1980 to promote technology-intensive R&D by domestic and international companies. By 1990 more than 100 companies were located there. As a result of this program, the Taiwanese government hopes that the country will have 50,000 people engaged in R&D by 1996. Through tax incentives and direct financial assistance, it intends to bring R&D spending up to 2.2 percent of GNP. To focus activity, the government has identified five "star" industries that are to be the mainstays of the technology drive:

- information

- consumer electronics

- telecommunications

- automation systems

- advanced materials

As part of this process, the government will also support the acquisition of foreign technology, marketing skills, raw materials, and environmental equipment.

Strategic Alliance Opportunities

Taiwan's export-oriented development strategy and tight controls on the financial sector have resulted in the accumulation of huge foreign exchange reserves. In 1991, Taiwan's reserves totalled $82 billion and could reach $100 billion by 1993. This glut of cash contributed to domestic inflationary pressures and provoked U.S. complaints about trade imbalances caused by unfair trading practices.

The Taiwanese government's program of economic and financial liberalization has been motivated, in part, by an effort to reduce these reserves by channeling them into productive investment abroad. The government has accordingly begun providing investment information as well as financial and technical assistance for companies seeking foreign investment opportunities.

As of April 1990, the Central Bank has been lending American dollars to Taiwanese enterprises through the Bank of Communications, the Export-Import

Bank, the International Commercial Bank of China, and the China Development Corporation, to cover up to 80 percent of the cost of investment projects abroad. The Bank of Communications has also opened a subsidiary in Amsterdam to help Taiwanese get a foothold in Europe.

Taiwanese FDI is flowing into a wide variety of sectors including food, textiles, leisure products, electronics, transportation, cement and construction, chemicals, hotels, banks, and brand-name consumer products. Taiwanese companies are using overseas investments to enhance their competitiveness and to:

* acquire new technologies;

* penetrate markets;

* set up international marketing networks;

* secure access to natural resources;

* establish business in politically stable regions;

* take advantage of the appreciation of Taiwanese currency; and

* take advantage of low labor costs to reduce production costs.

Initially, the largest Taiwanese corporations dominated outward investment. As Taiwan's economic difficulties increase, however, small and medium-sized enterprises in labor-intensive industries are becoming the major source of outbound investment.

Joint ventures are particularly attractive for these smaller companies, since local partners can orient them and provide them with market intelligence and expertise. Both U.S. products and U.S. companies are well regarded, and this visibility is compounded by a concerted Taiwanese effort to "buy American" in order to reduce Taiwan's trade surpluses with the United States. Taiwanese are very loyal to a product once they accept it, and U.S. products have developed an advantage in the marketplace. As of 1992, by way of contrast, Canada had not yet emerged as a significant destination for Taiwanese foreign direct investment: Canada and Canadian companies remain little known to Taiwanese business people and consumers.

Having invested heavily in Southeast Asia, Taiwanese companies are looking more closely at the whole North American market. Taiwanese investors are particularly interested in technology-intensive areas such as computer hardware and software, high-precision electronic components and systems, medical instruments, environmental equipment, telecommunications, transportation technology, machinery, aerospace components, integrated financial services, biotechnology and pharmaceuticals.

North American firms with technology in these areas are likely to find Taiwan to be a good source of capital, and able to provide manufacturing facilities and effective market access to the Pacific Rim region.

Environmental equipment is another large area of opportunity. Taiwan will invest $38 billion in pollution control and waste disposal by the year 2000, and the country is actively looking for partners in this area. Companies dealing in air pollution, water pollution, and solid waste management equipment are all needed.

Negotiating in Taiwan

Taiwan displays many traditional Chinese cultural attributes. Unlike Hong Kong and Singapore, however, it lacks a British connection, and outside the business community relatively few Taiwanese speak English.

As elsewhere in Asia, business cards are absolutely essential. They are even exchanged in social settings. Your business cards should be translated into Mandarin.

Authority in Taiwan is based on status and age. Unlike Japan, consensus decision-making is not part of the Taiwanese system of management. The directives of superiors are seldom questioned, and many family-controlled businesses are headed by a patriarch who is the unquestioned decision-maker.

When meeting Taiwanese business people, a slight bow of the head and a handshake are appropriate. Elderly persons are always recognized and greeted first.

Proposed Areas for Future Strategic Alliances

- electronic components and systems

- automotive parts

- civilian aircraft components

- environmental protection equipment

- computer and communications equipment and software

- biotechnology and pharmaceuticals

- material sciences

- integrated financial services

Source: Ministry of Economic Affairs, Taiwan.

CHAPTER 19

DOING BUSINESS IN THE ASIA-PACIFIC REGION

- LANGUAGE
- RELATIVE VALUE
- LAWYERS AND LEGAL DOCUMENTS
- FORMS OF ADDRESS AND BUSINESS CARDS
- YOUR PRESENTATION

The vast cultural gulf between East and West can be difficult to bridge. North American companies may have to work harder to make alliances with Asia-Pacific firms work, than they would with a European partner. After all, North American corporate structures, business practices, and accounting procedures—not to mention languages—all have their roots in Europe.

Partnering with Asian firms often means adapting to unfamiliar industry standards, strange social and business practices, different management styles, and unusual corporate outlooks.

Understanding the Differences

When Britain's Celltech entered into drug development alliances with the American firm Cyanamid and Japan's Sankyo, Celltech found it had to work "three or four times as hard" on relations with its Japanese partner, said Celltech chief executive officer Gerard Fairclough. "Communications take longer because of [national] and medical practice differences. We've had to put in more effort than we planned." [1]

There are many obvious and not-so-obvious differences between North American and Asian cultures. Recognizing these differences and overcoming cultural barriers is vital to negotiating and managing successful alliances in the Asia-Pacific region.

Language

Communicating with business people from the Asia-Pacific region requires overcoming different cultural viewpoints as well as the language barrier. For example, the Australians speak English, but they use it in subtly different ways. Unless you pay attention to the cultural nuances embedded in their usage, you may miss something important.

The problem is much greater when dealing with business people whose first language is not English, or who do not speak English at all. Even when the words you and your negotiating partner are exchanging have been smoothly and correctly translated, the intended meaning may not have been communicated. When a Japanese businessman hesitates and responds to your request with "that may be difficult," what he is really telling you is "no."

Of course, the services of a good translator are vital. Translating your proposition into the language of your hosts is both an important courtesy and a practical aid. Avoid using North American business jargon such as "the bottom line," or clichés such as "lean and mean." And remember, when your opposite number nods and smiles, that does not necessarily mean he or she understands you.

In your discussions you will need sensitivity, patience, and politeness. As you talk, pause frequently, and offer to answer questions. Encourage your prospective partners to confer among themselves. Create the impression, however difficult it may be, that time means nothing to you, and that your only mission is to communicate fully and honestly.

---

1   Michael Gerlach, "Business Alliances and the Strategy of the Japanese Firm," *California Management Review*, Fall 1987, p. 126.

Relative Values

The goals of Asian business people tend to be somewhat more complex that those of North American business people. Obviously, both are interested in profits, but the Asians are also keenly interested in long-term benefits.

For example, a McKinsey & Company study of 90 mid-level managers at 25 leading Japanese companies found that 85 percent thought entering new businesses or improving the position of existing ones was more important than financial gain. This is in sharp contract to the profit orientation of many Western executives.

Most Western business people think in terms of quarter-to-quarter results, and two years is considered a distant horizon for a business. Business people in Asia, however, think in terms of 5, 10, or even 20-year spans. That is why they prefer to proceed slowly in negotiations: once a commitment is made, it will be with them for a long time.

Asian business people will therefore use the first few meetings simply to get to know you and determine if you are the kind of person with whom they want to do business. They are looking for stable business relationships with trustworthy and compatible people.

Many North American business people get frustrated by the slow pace and seeming complexity of negotiations in Asia. There may be a lot of people involved in making the decisions on the other side, and you may not even have a clear idea of who the key players are.

In North American companies, decisions tend to be made by a small group of people who must then seek internal agreement before their strategy can be implemented. In many of the Asian countries, especially Japan, the people who will implement the policy have already been included in the decision-making process.

Lawyers and Legal Documents

Business people in Asia rely on personal understanding and trust rather than on formal contracts. For this reason, most Asians would be offended if you brought a lawyer along to a meeting: it would be as if you had brought a policeman, and could create an atmosphere of distrust, killing negotiations before they start.

To satisfy your people at home, you will eventually need some sort of written agreement, but keep it as simple as possible, and do not bring it to the table until the negotiations are complete. If your Asian partner has doubts about the negotiations, no legal document will salvage the deal.

Forms of Address and Business Cards

When addressing people within their own cultures, Japanese, Koreans, and ethnic Chinese place their family name first. But when they are speaking English or dealing with Western business people, they follow the Western usage with the family name last, after the given names.

This usage will be observed on the English side of their business cards, too. Always use the person's family name, preceded by an appropriate title such as Mr., Mrs., Miss, or Doctor. Often a business title such as Director is also appropriate. Do not use first names unless invited to do so.

Your Presentation

Your presentation is the key to explaining what you propose and what you are looking for. When preparing it, include as many visuals as you can, since they are the best way of overcoming communications barriers. The visual presentation should tell the whole story and should be comprehensible even to those who do not speak English. Use English for your labels and headings, however; otherwise you will convey the false impression that you speak the language.

Transparencies for overhead projectors are the best medium for presentation. They are easy to carry and require less equipment than slides. Almost every office has an overhead projector or can readily get one (but make sure before your meeting). Have the transparencies prepared professionally, and avoid a hard sell that might smack of Western advertising.

When it comes to knowing your subject, you cannot prepare too carefully. Asian business people have an insatiable appetite for detail.

Next to a strong visual presentation, a comprehensive briefing book is your most valuable tool. It should take the form of a loose-leaf binder with subject areas segregated by tabs.

If you and your staff prepare it properly, no question will stump you. Also, as you make your presentations, you can add to the book based on the questions that your audiences poses to you.

A STRATEGIC AUDIT

Deciding whether an alliance will satisfy your strategic objectives demands a thorough analysis of your present situation. Here is an analysis of strengths, weaknesses, opportunities, and threats (SWOT) that can help you determine the present position of your firm in each of its business segments.

Market Analysis

1. What is your present market position? Consider product life cycle, market share, price of product, quality, marketing strategy, market research skills, patents, licenses, and agreements.

2. What are the current industry trends? How does your firm fit in? What are your direct and indirect competitors doing? (price, quality, originality)

3. What are your market opportunities?

   a. What would you like to do?

4. How effective are your dealer/distribution and service networks and do they need improvement?

5. How flexible is your current corporate structure?

   a. What changes could be made? (production, personnel, training, equipment)

6. What are your promotional and marketing strategies and how effective have they been?

Innovation

1. What is your assessment of your current R&D situation?

   a. Any recent successes?

   b. Were these commercial successes?

   c. What are your in-house R&D capabilities?

   d. What are your competitors doing in product research, process research, and technology imitation?

2. Is your staff creative, qualified, reliable, and productive?

3. What patents do you have and what do they cover?

   a. How dated is the technology?

4. What licenses has your company bought and how are they used?

    a.   How much do they cost?

    b.   How dated is the technology?

5.   Could you access outside sources of research or technical human resources? Consider suppliers, customers, and contractors.

6.   What is the relationship between your R&D activities and your marketing strategy?

Productivity

1.   Is your firm taking advantage of economies of scale?

2.   Are you using appropriate technology?

    a.   Is it your technology?

    b.   What are the cost advantages?

3.   How flexible or integrated is your production process?

    a.   At what capacity are you operating?

    b.   Is there room for expansion?

    c.   How effective are your quality control processes?

4.   Consider issues related to labor force, plant location, transportation costs, as well as access to and cost of raw materials.

5. What are your competitors doing?

Financial Resources

1. Are your present financial resources sufficient to meet your present objectives? (R&D, marketing, sales, promotion, training)

   a. Do you have cash flow problems?

   b. What is your present equity position?

2. What is your borrowing capacity in both the short- and the long-term?

3. How are your finances being managed?

4. How important are issues like fluctuating exchange rates, transfer pricing, dividends, the repatriation of funds?

5. Are there any changes that you would like to make to your management and financial accounting systems?

Profitability

1. What is your company's five-year trend in profitability?

   a. How does this compare to the industry average?

   b. How does it compare to your competitors?

2. What are the trends in prices and margins for your product?

Human Resources

1. Rate current management on the following issues:

    a. Leadership

    b. Ability to motivate others

    c. Ability to coordinate departments, divisions or functions

    d. Flexibility and adaptability

2. What are the leadership and motivational qualities of your CEO?

3. Are there managers experienced in managing acquisitions, mergers, joint ventures, or any form of strategic alliance?

4. Do your managers have international business experience?

5. What kind of attention do you pay to training and development for your staff?

6. Consider employee morale and commitment to the company. What incentives do they have?

7. How skilled is your work force?

8. What is the average age of the work force in relation to that of management?

Selecting an appropriate partner takes time and resources. Identify clearly and precisely the specific venture to be pursued and what is expected from your partner—and make this known to your prospects. Frank and open communication with your partner is important.

Don't be misled by superficial similarities between you and your potential partner. Take a look at the prospect's balance sheet, financial stability, plans for growth, and profit orientation. And if the partner is an unknown, start small and build from there.

Capability

1. What are the competitive strengths and weaknesses of your partner? It may be wise to develop a pre-incorporation agreement identifying the various strengths each of you can bring to the table and what each firm will contribute to the alliance.

2. Do your technical skills and resources complement each other?

3. Does your partner have sufficient financial resources? This issue is especially important if the alliance depends on the partner's financial contribution.

4. Does your partner have management resources of sufficient quality and depth to coordinate with you and to administer its share of the alliance?

5. Is there sufficient symmetry between your two firms to form the basis for complementarity? Large firms have a tendency to impose their management culture and corporate demands on smaller companies.

6. Do you have sufficient bargaining leverage to reduce the risk of your partner demanding far more than it gives to the venture?

Objectives

1. What are your partner's real motivations?

2. How critical is the proposed alliance to your partner's long-term business strategy?

a. Does your partner need the venture in order to meet its own tactical and strategic objectives?

b. What resources is your partner willing to commit to the alliance?

c. Is there a champion inside the other firm who will strive to ensure the success of the alliance?

3. Are the time horizons you want acceptable to the other side?

4. Are the expected returns clearly understood?

5. Is your potential partner in direct competition with you? If so, in which markets?

Chemistry

1. Are your business cultures and attitudes compatible?

2. What is your partner's orientation toward risk and profit?

3. Are your operating policies compatible?

4. Are your management teams compatible?

5. What is your partner's track record on cooperation?

Protection

1. Are there measures in place to protect your contribution (e.g., proprietary technology)?

2. Do you know the intellectual property laws in force in the prospect's country?

3. What measures can you take to guard against unfair appropriation of your know-how?

4. What do people who have already partnered in the country have to say about their experience there?

5. What are the various legal risks regarding competition in the market you are entering?

THE ELEMENTS OF A JOINT-VENTURE AGREEMENT

A. Organization and Structure of the Joint Venture

1. The scope of the joint venture and arrangements for expansion:
   a. specifically identified development projects;
   b. general cooperation with future identification of projects;
   c. the goals of each member should be specifically ascertained.

2. Type of business organization to be selected as joint-venture vehicle.

B. Financing the Joint Venture

1. Amount of initial capital required and how it will be supplied, i.e, money or assets.

2. Means of financing additional working capital and expenses—bank borrowings, including guaranties, and mandatory or optional additional capital contributions.

3. Consequences of default in making additional mandatory contributions ("dilution" provisions).

4. How proposals for expansion will be handled. Consequences of failure to agree, consequences of voluntary contributions.

5. Sharing of profits and losses, based on ownership share, capital contribution, stipulated percentage.

6. Sharing of liabilities—joint or several. Cost of defense of claims.

7. Appointment of accountants, establishment of accounting procedures;
   a. keeping of and access to books and records by parties;
   b. designation of fiscal year;
   c. bank accounts.

8. Salaries, if any.

C. Management and Control of the Joint Venture

1. Voting rights.

2. Identity, method of selection, and powers and responsibilities of key managerial personnel and their successors.

3. Size and constitution of board of directors, management committee or its counterpart, as appropriate.
   a. Method of decision-making by board (unanimous, majority, or otherwise).

4. Methods of breaking deadlocks (arbitration, buyout or auction, liquidation provisions).

5. Venture policy is determined ordinarily through boards of directors or management committees, as appropriate.

6. Activities that may require formal action (new development programs, levels of production, annual budgets, acquisition or surrender of property, claim settlements, guarantees, and other similar matters).

7. Transfer of ownership interest (rights of first refusal, exemptions with respect to affiliates, continuing obligations and liabilities of affiliates, appraisal provisions in event of disagreement).

8. Preemptive rights.

D. Employees of the Joint Venture

1. Choice of employees.

2. Establishment of general standards for operator (due diligence, workmanlike manner, reasonableness, good faith.)

3. Compensation of employees.

4. Consequence of breach.

5 Removal proceedings, right to terminate agreement, choice of successor.

E. Marketing of Joint-Venture Product

1. Responsibility for marketing decisions (management committee or board of directors, unanimous vote of members, or discretion of employee).

2. Joint marketing; note antitrust issues.

3. Product supply agreements.

4. Development program—master plan and initial plan.

F. Restrictions on Activities of Members of Joint Venture

1. Competition within specified territory during and subsequent to joint venture.

2. General confidentiality provisions covering all information received in connection with joint venture.

3. "Area-of-interest" provision: any property or interest or other business opportunity acquired by any party to the joint venture or any affiliate thereof must be offered to the joint venture on the same terms and conditions as it was acquired.

4. "Competition" clause: except with respect to joint venture property or area of interest, parties are free to compete as if the joint venture did not exist (limitation of fiduciary duty created by joint venture).

5. Provision for reacquisition by parties of surrendered joint-venture property; only parties not involved in disposition may reacquire for own account.

G. Default by Members of Joint Venture

1. Definition of defaults.

2. Consequences of default (monetary penalties, forfeitures, waivers of certain rights, termination of joint venture and others). It is important to have different penalties for different defaults.

3. Indemnification upon default.

H. Proprietary Rights

1. Any special arrangements for supplying patent rights and know-how to the joint venture by members. Need for licensing agreements.

2. Provisions relating to use of trademarks, if any.

3. Provisions relating to disclosure of improvements.

I. Term and Termination of Joint Venture

1. Specify commencement of term. Should be subject to regulatory approvals obtained and other conditions met.

2. Specify:
    a. duration of term;
    b. method of termination or prior agreement to terminate;
    c. method of renewal;
    d. penalties for wrongful withdrawal;
    e. consequences of bankruptcy, death of certainparties and other events.

3. "Hardship Reopener": the provision that allows for modification or termination of the joint venture in the event of financial hardship to a member or the operation of the joint venture on "non-economic" basis.

4. a. Disposition of assets upon termination, including options to purchase assets, division of proceeds of assets, and buy out provisions.
    b. Method of evaluation of terminating party's interest.

J. Miscellaneous Considerations

1. Governing law provision.

2. Force majeure provision.

3. Modifications and waivers of joint-venture agreements.

4. Arbitration of disputes.

K. Documentation of the Joint Venture

The first step in negotiation of a joint venture is usually the preparation of a brief outline of the basic terms of the proposal. This outline, or memorandum of understanding (MOU), is usually not intended as a binding document, but rather as an expression of mutual intent with respect to the basic features of the transaction. The outline provides the basis for the detailed negotiations and for the drafting of the formal joint-venture documents.

The specific arrangements concerning the establishment and operation of the joint venture are normally set forth in a joint-venture agreement, which covers all aspects of the partnership in detail.

Additional documentation may include:

- the organizational documents of the joint-venture vehicle;

- patent, know-how, or trademark license agreements;

- technical assistance agreements;

- leases;

- construction contracts;

- management contracts;

- employment contracts for key personnel.

INDEX

D

About the Editors

Marvin V. Bedward is the President of Prospectus Investment and Trade Partners Inc. and the managing director for The Prospectus Group, a Canadian-based publishing and consultancy group providing business information, business tools, and advice for international business development and community economic development. Mr. Bedward has provided marketing and investment advice to North American and European companies seeking to do business in Canada and the U.S. He has worked with companies in U.S., Japan, U.K. and Canada to develop licensing agreements and locate potential partners for strategic alliances. As former senior advisor and manager in the Canadian federal government, he helped develop the investment promotion strategy for Investment Canada and the Department of Industry, Science and Technology. Mr. Bedward holds degrees in business from the University of Ottawa.

Mark V. Anderson was born in St. Paul, MN. He graduated from Carleton Univestiy in Ottawa, Canada, with an honors degree in English Literature. Mr. Anderson is currently working as a business writer/journalist based in Canada's national capital Ottawa. He specializes in writing and reporting on such topics as export development for small- and medium-sized companies, business-labor relations, government policy and issues of international competitiveness.

The Prospectus Group of Companies are Canadian-based publishing and consulting companies specializing in business research, publications and management consultancy on issues of international business development, trade, investment, communications, human resources and government relations. Prospectus clients include companies specializing in the energy, medical, construction and information technologies sectors, as well as government departments of industry, trade, environment and economic development in Canada, Australia, Poland Hungary and Venezuela.

Writers

Dr. Jan Fedorowicz is a specialist in international business development for small– and medium–sized business. He has written quite extensively on trade and investment issues, including books on doing business in Canada, Poland, Asia Pacific and an upcoming publication on business opportunities in Mexico. Prior to assuming his present duties as President of Prospectus Publications Ltd., he has been a professor, a broadcaster, a manager of international trade for a major business association, senior writer/editor in a leading Canadian corporation and senior partner in a research and consulting firm.

Dr. Michael Kelly writes and lectures extensively on international business strategy issues. He currently lectures in the MBA program at the University of Ottawa and is in adjunct Research Professor at Carlton University's School of Business.

Mr. Arpad Abonyi, M.A. is a specialist in international investment and technology. He is the author of a number of publications on investment promotion, strategic alliances and doing business in Europe 1992 and Hungary. Mr. Abonyi is president of Okus International Inc., a business consulting firm advising companies which are entering the Hungarian market.

Mr. William Gaynor, B.A. is a writer/researcher on issues dealing with investment, strategic alliances and general business issues. He is co-authored publications on Europe 1992 and strategic alliances.

Research Associates

Dr. Lynn Mytelka
Ms. Katie Reid, B.A.
Ms. Dyna Vynk Ellis, M.A.

About the Publisher

PROBUS PUBLISHING COMPANY

Probus Publishing Company fills the informational needs of today's business professional by publishing authoritative, quality books on timely and relevant topics, including:

- Investing
- Futures/Options Trading
- Banking
- Finance
- Marketing and Sales
- Manufacturing and Project Management
- Personal Finance, Real Estate, Insurance and Estate Planning
- Entrepreneurship
- Management

Probus books are available at quantity discounts when purchased for business, educational or sales promotional use. For more information, please call the Director, Corporate/Institutional Sales at 1-800-PROBUS-1, or write:

Director, Corporate/Institutional Sales
Probus Publishing Company
1925 N. Clybourn Avenue
Chicago, Illinois 60614
FAX (312) 868-6250